S0-AHX-568

Jack the Ripper

A Journal of the Whitechapel Murders
1888 – 1889

ADAPTED BY
Rick Geary

"MURDER IS STALKING RED-HANDED 'MID THE HOMES OF THE WEARY POOR."

FROM A POEM PUBLISHED IN
REYNOLDS NEWSPAPER, 1888

"WELL, SUPPOSE I DO GET KILLED, IT WILL BE A GOOD THING FOR ME, FOR THE WINTER IS COMING ON, AND THE LIFE IS AWFUL."

A WHITECHAPEL PROSTITUTE

"...THE ASSASSIN, IF NOT SUFFERING FROM INSANITY, APPEARS TO BE FREE FROM ANY FEAR OF INTERRUPTION WHILE AT HIS DREADFUL WORK."

THE LONDON TIMES
1 OCTOBER 1888

Also available by Geary:
A Treasury of Victorian Murder Compendium:
hc.: $24.99
A Treasury of Victorian Murder:
Vol. I, pb.: $9.95, E-book: $6.99
The Fatal Bullet, pb.: $9.95
E-book: $6.99
The Borden Tragedy, $9.99
The Mystery of Mary Rogers, hc.: $15.95
The Beast of Chicago pb.: $9.95, E-book: $6.99
The Murder of Abraham Lincoln
pb.: $9.95, hc.: $15.95, E-book: $6.99
The Case of Madeleine Smith
pb.: $8.95, hc.: $15.95
The Bloody Benders
pb.: $9.95, hc.: $15.95, E-book: $6.99
A Treasury of XXth Century Murder:
The Lindbergh Child
pb.: $9.95, hc.: $15.95, E-book: $6.99
Famous Players
pb.: $9.95, hc.: $15.95, E-book: $6.99
The Axe-Man of New Orleans
hc.: $15.99, E-book: $6.99
The Lives of Sacco & Vanzetti, hc.: $15.99
Lovers Lane, hc.: $15.99

See more on these
at our website:
www.nbmpublishing.com

P&H: $4 1st item, $1 each addt'l.

We have over 200 titles,
write for our color catalog:
NBM
160 Broadway, Suite 700, East Wing,
New York, NY 10038

ISBN 13: 978-1-56163-308-1
©1995 Rick Geary

Fifth Printing

Comicslit is an imprint
and trademark of

NANTIER · BEALL · MINOUSTCHINE
Publishing inc.
new york

INTRODUCTION

This account of the "Jack the Ripper" murders is compiled from the journals of an unknown British gentleman who lived in London during 1888-1889 and closely followed the increasingly savage killings. An obvious crime buff and armchair detective, he apparently had contacts within the Metropolitan and City police departments which enabled him to receive information before its release to the general public. The journals (amounting to twenty-four volumes) have been authenticated as dating from the late Victorian era, and the facts within have been checked against the known records of the "Ripper" atrocities.

BIBLIOGRAPHY

The historical information in the journals has been checked against the following sources:
Begg, Paul, Martin Fido and Keith Skinner, *The Jack the Ripper A to Z.* (Headline Book Publishing, 1994)
Chesney, Kellow, *The Victorian Underworld.* (Pelican Books, 1979)
Harrison, Shirley and Michael Barrett, *The Diary of Jack the Ripper.* (Hyperion, 1993)
Infamous Murders. (Verdict Press, 1975)
Knight, Stephen, *Jack the Ripper, the Final Solution.* (George C. Harrap and Co., 1976)
The London Times, 10 August - 23 November, 1888, reprinted in *The Fatal Caress,*
Richard Barker, ed. (Duell, Sloan and Pierce, 1947)
McGowran, Bill, "Jack The Ripper: Eight Theories. "*The Mammoth Book of Murder,*
Richard Glyn Jones, ed. (Carroll and Graf, 1989)
Pearsall, Ronald, *The Worm in the Bud: the World of Victorian Sexuality.* (Penguin Books, 1983)
Perry, George and Nicholas Mason, *The Victorians: A World Built to Last.* (Viking Press, 1974)
Rumbelow, Donald, *The Complete Jack the Ripper:* (New York Graphic Society, 1975)
Revised and updated edition (Berkley Books, 1990)
Wilson, Colin, "My Search for Jack the Ripper." reprinted in *Solved*, Richard Glyn Jones, ed. (Peter Bedrick Books, 1987)
Wilson, Colin, "The 'Ripper' Mystery." *True Crime 2*, Damon Wilson, ed. (Carroll and Graf, 1990)

· 1888 ·
WHITECHAPEL
and the
CRIMES of
Jack the Ripper

MARY ANN NICHOLS
31 AUGUST

ELIZABETH STRIDE
30 SEPTEMBER

ANNIE CHAPMAN
8 SEPTEMBER

MARY JANE KELLY
9 NOVEMBER

CATHERINE EDDOWES
30 SEPTEMBER

MYSTERIOUS
CHALK INSCRIPTION
30 SEPTEMBER

BUCK'S ROW

LONDON HOSPITAL

NEW ROAD

WHITECHAPEL

THE COMMERCIAL ROAD

BERNER ST.

WHITECHAPEL HIGH STREET

BRICK LANE

HANBURY ST.

COMMERCIAL STREET

LEMAN ST.

GOULSTON ST.

PORSET ST.

MIDDLESEX ST.

CITY OF LONDON

HOUNDSDITCH

BISHOPSGATE

DUKE ST.

MITRE SQ.

ALDGATE

LEADENHALL ST.

MINORIES

THE TOWER

1888

FRIDAY 31 AUGUST

A SHOCKING MURDER ON THE EAST END. I'M TOLD THAT THE BODY OF A WOMAN WAS FOUND THIS MORNING IN A SQUALID ALLEY-WAY OF THE WHITECHAPEL DISTRICT... MUTILATED IN A MOST HORRIFYING MANNER —

A PORTER ON HIS WAY TO WORK PASSED DOWN BUCK'S ROW AT ABOUT 3:40 A.M. HE NOTICED A DARK BUNDLE ON THE OPPOSITE SIDE-WALK.

VENTURING CLOSER, HE SAW IT TO BE A WOMAN, RECLINING PEACEFULLY... WAS SHE MERELY UNCONSCIOUS?

THE NEAREST POLICE OFFICER WAS SUMMONED: CONSTABLE JOHN NEILL. HIS LAMP REVEALED THAT THE POOR WOMAN WAS DEAD OF A CUT THROAT!

THE CONSTABLE, IT SEEMS, HAD PATROLLED THIS VERY STREET NO MORE THAN THIRTY MINUTES EARLIER...AT THAT TIME, IT HAD BEEN QUIET AND EMPTY.

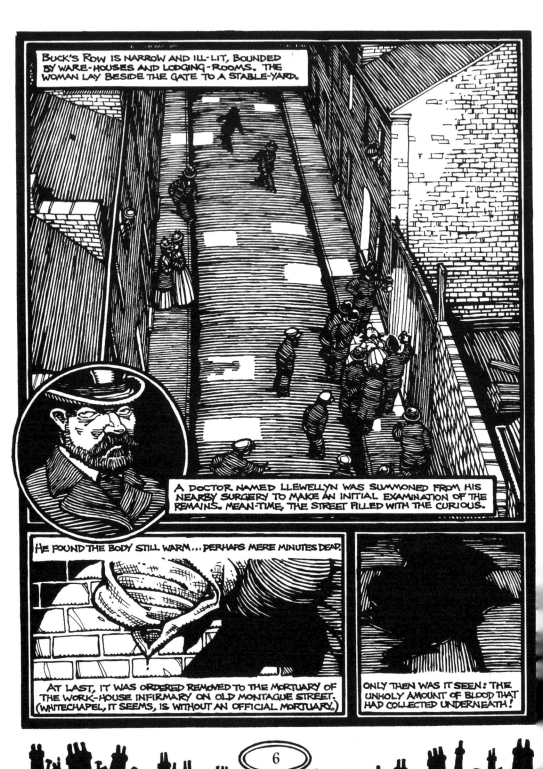

BUCK'S ROW IS NARROW AND ILL-LIT, BOUNDED BY WARE-HOUSES AND LODGING-ROOMS. THE WOMAN LAY BESIDE THE GATE TO A STABLE-YARD.

A DOCTOR NAMED LLEWELLYN WAS SUMMONED FROM HIS NEARBY SURGERY TO MAKE AN INITIAL EXAMINATION OF THE REMAINS. MEAN-TIME, THE STREET FILLED WITH THE CURIOUS.

HE FOUND THE BODY STILL WARM... PERHAPS MERE MINUTES DEAD.

AT LAST, IT WAS ORDERED REMOVED TO THE MORTUARY OF THE WORK-HOUSE INFIRMARY ON OLD MONTAGUE STREET. (WHITECHAPEL, IT SEEMS, IS WITHOUT AN OFFICIAL MORTUARY.)

ONLY THEN WAS IT SEEN: THE UNHOLY AMOUNT OF BLOOD THAT HAD COLLECTED UNDERNEATH!

LATER IN THE MORNING, DR. LLEWELLYN PERFORMED A THOROUGH POST-MORTEM. THESE ARE HIS FINDINGS:

THE WOMAN — AGED ABOUT 45 YEARS — SUSTAINED TWO DEEP SLASHES TO THE THROAT ... AND FURTHER INJURIES NOT NOTED AT THE MURDER SCENE:

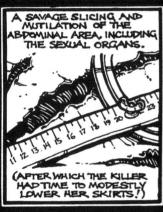
A SAVAGE SLICING AND MUTILATION OF THE ABDOMINAL AREA, INCLUDING THE SEXUAL ORGANS.

(AFTER WHICH THE KILLER HAD TIME TO MODESTLY LOWER HER SKIRTS!)

SEVERAL BRUISES ABOUT THE FACE SEEM TO INDICATE THAT SHE HAD FIRST BEEN RENDERED UNCONSCIOUS.

THE DEED WAS APPARENTLY COMMITTED WITH A STOUT-HANDLED BLADE OF SIX TO EIGHT INCHES ...

SUCH AS A CORK-CUTTER OR SHOE-MAKER MIGHT USE!

THE WOUNDS WERE INFLICTED LEFT-TO-RIGHT, LEADING THE DOCTOR TO FURTHER SURMISE THAT THE MURDERER IS LEFT-HANDED ...

THIS ASSUMES, OF COURSE, THAT THE VICTIM WAS SET-UPON AND SLASHED FROM THE FRONT.

SOME WOMEN FROM THE NEIGHBOURHOOD WERE BROUGHT IN TO IDENTIFY THE DECEASED: A LOCAL RESIDENT THEY KNOW ONLY AS "POLLY."

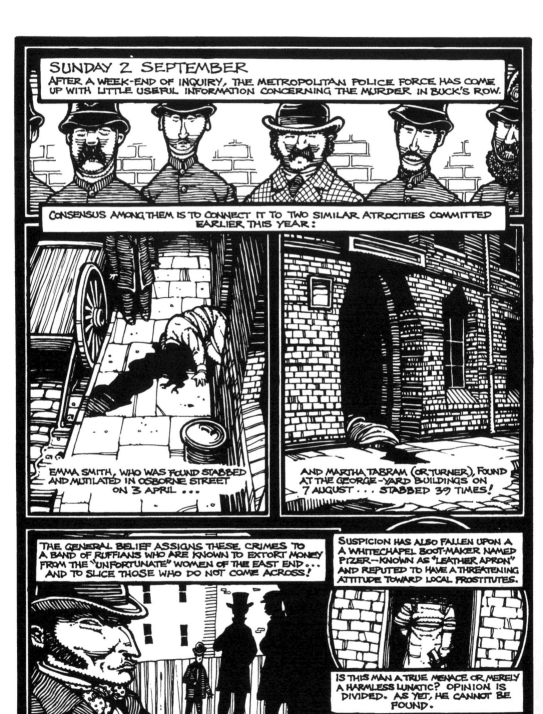

SUNDAY 2 SEPTEMBER

AFTER A WEEK-END OF INQUIRY, THE METROPOLITAN POLICE FORCE HAS COME UP WITH LITTLE USEFUL INFORMATION CONCERNING THE MURDER IN BUCK'S ROW.

CONSENSUS AMONG THEM IS TO CONNECT IT TO TWO SIMILAR ATROCITIES COMMITTED EARLIER THIS YEAR:

EMMA SMITH, WHO WAS FOUND STABBED AND MUTILATED IN OSBORNE STREET ON 3 APRIL...

AND MARTHA TABRAM (OR TURNER), FOUND AT THE GEORGE-YARD BUILDINGS ON 7 AUGUST... STABBED 39 TIMES!

THE GENERAL BELIEF ASSIGNS THESE CRIMES TO A BAND OF RUFFIANS WHO ARE KNOWN TO EXTORT MONEY FROM THE "UNFORTUNATE" WOMEN OF THE EAST END... AND TO SLICE THOSE WHO DO NOT COME ACROSS!

SUSPICION HAS ALSO FALLEN UPON A A WHITECHAPEL BOOT-MAKER NAMED PIZER—KNOWN AS "LEATHER APRON" AND REPUTED TO HAVE A THREATENING ATTITUDE TOWARD LOCAL PROSTITUTES.

IS THIS MAN A TRUE MENACE OR MERELY A HARMLESS LUNATIC? OPINION IS DIVIDED. AS YET, HE CANNOT BE FOUND.

MY SUSPICION, HOWEVER, IS THAT SUCH MUNDANE EXPLANATIONS WILL NOT ACCOUNT FOR THE SAVAGERY OF THIS MURDER... WHICH SEEMS NOT THE WORK OF YOUR EVERY-DAY CRIMINAL TYPE.

THE DISTRICT OF WHITECHAPEL HAS LONG BEEN HAVEN TO THE DEGRADED AND DISPOSSESSED OF THIS AND EVERY OTHER NATION OF THE WORLD...

WHERE EVEN UNDER ORDINARY CONDITIONS, ONE MAY WITNESS THE LOWEST LEVELS OF HUMAN VENALITY AND PERVERSION.

THE ENTIRE EAST END IS VICTIM TO OVER-CROWDING, BAD SANITATION AND UNIMAGINABLE POVERTY.

I AM TOLD THAT FEWER THAN HALF THE CHILDREN BORN WILL LIVE TO SEE THE AGE OF FIVE.

IT IS A STATE OF AFFAIRS OF WHICH NO ENGLISHMAN IS PROUD... NOR SHOULD ALLOW TO FURTHER ENDURE!

A STRONG MAN CAN FIND EMPLOYMENT IN THE SLAUGHTER-YARDS OF ALDGATE . . .

OR CARTING AND LOADING AT THE DOCKS OR MARKETS . . . EARNING PERHAPS TWENTY SHILLINGS PER WEEK.

THE WOMEN ALSO WORK IN THE MARKETS OR AT SCRUBBING AND WASHING AND NEEDLE-WORK . . .

AND ALL-TOO-OFTEN, WHEN NOTHING ELSE PRESENTS ITSELF, THEY WILL END UP SELLING "FAVOURS" TO MEN.

DENIZENS OF THE STREETS AND ALLEY-WAYS CAN FIND A VERMIN-RIDDEN BED IN A "DOSS" HOUSE FOR FOUR-PENCE PER NIGHT.

BUT MANY SIMPLY CURL UP IN A DOORWAY OR STRETCH OUT IN A GUTTER.

The Queen's Head

WHAT-EVER EXCESS INCOME PEOPLE MIGHT POSSESS IS SPENT ON DRINK . . . WHICH IS CHEAP AND PLENTIFUL THROUGH-OUT THE EAST END.

IN THE QUIET AND SAFETY OF MY STUDY, IT BECOMES ALL-TOO-EASY TO MORALIZE AGAINST THESE OUTCASTS . . .

BUT ALL OF US MIGHT PROFITABLY ASK OURSELVES: "WHAT WOULD I DO TO SURVIVE?"

MONDAY 3 SEPTEMBER
THE INQUEST OVER THE REMAINS OF THE BUCK'S ROW VICTIM OPENED THIS MORNING AT THE WORKING LAD'S INSTITUTE ON WHITECHAPEL RD. UNDER THE DIRECTION OF THE CORONER, MR. WYNN E. BAXTER.

THE UNFORTUNATE WOMAN HAS BEEN IDENTIFIED AS MARY ANN (OR "POLLY") NICHOLS ... AGED 42 YEARS ... A COMMON STREET PROSTITUTE.

IN HER POCKETS HAD BEEN FOUND HER ONLY POSSESSIONS.

HER ESTRANGED HUSBAND, A PRINTER, TESTIFIED THAT SHE WAS THE MOTHER OF FIVE ...

BUT THEY HAD BEEN LIVING APART FOR SEVERAL YEARS, DUE TO HER HABITUAL DRUNKENNESS.

DURING THAT TIME, SHE HAD LIVED AT WORK-HOUSES IN LAMBETH AND HOLBORN AND EDMONTON ...

AND, UNTIL RECENTLY, IN A LODGING-HOUSE AT 18 THRAWL ST.

HER HUSBAND, AS HE GAZED AT THE PITIFUL REMAINS, COULD BE HEARD TO WHISPER: " I FORGIVE YOU FOR EVERYTHING, NOW THAT I SEE YOU LIKE THIS."

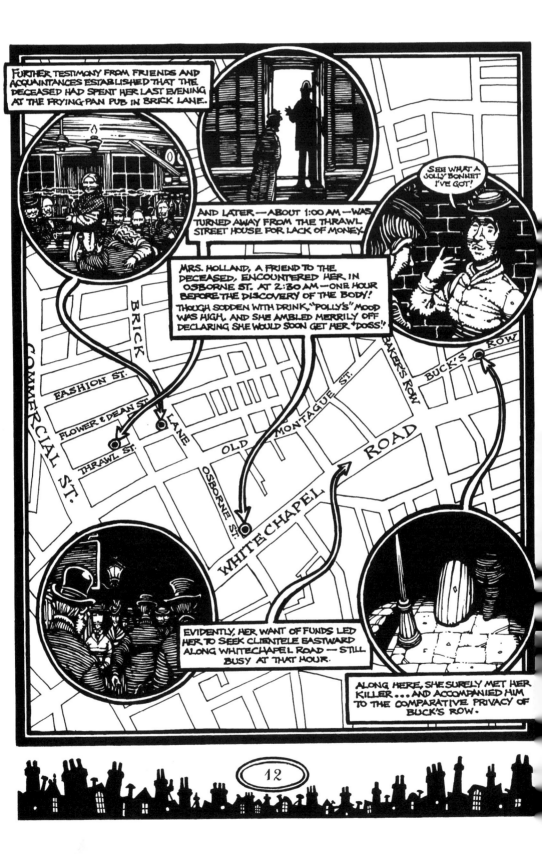

FURTHER TESTIMONY FROM FRIENDS AND ACQUAINTANCES ESTABLISHED THAT THE DECEASED HAD SPENT HER LAST EVENING AT THE FRYING-PAN PUB IN BRICK LANE.

AND LATER — ABOUT 1:00 AM — WAS TURNED AWAY FROM THE THRAWL STREET HOUSE FOR LACK OF MONEY.

SEE WHAT A JOLLY BONNET I'VE GOT!

MRS. HOLLAND, A FRIEND TO THE DECEASED, ENCOUNTERED HER IN OSBORNE ST. AT 2:30 AM — ONE HOUR BEFORE THE DISCOVERY OF THE BODY! THOUGH SODDEN WITH DRINK, "POLLY'S" MOOD WAS HIGH, AND SHE AMBLED MERRILY OFF DECLARING SHE WOULD SOON GET HER "DOSS"!

EVIDENTLY, HER WANT OF FUNDS LED HER TO SEEK CLIENTELE EASTWARD ALONG WHITECHAPEL ROAD — STILL BUSY AT THAT HOUR.

ALONG HERE, SHE SURELY MET HER KILLER ... AND ACCOMPANIED HIM TO THE COMPARATIVE PRIVACY OF BUCK'S ROW.

BRICK LANE

COMMERCIAL ST.

FASHION ST.

FLOWER & DEAN ST.

THRAWL ST.

OSBORNE ST.

OLD MONTAGUE ST.

BAKER'S ROW

BUCK'S ROW

WHITECHAPEL ROAD

TWO LADIES WHO LIVE ON BUCKS ROW: MRS. GREEN...

AND MRS. PURKISS...

INDEED, THERE IS MUCH SPECULATION OVER HOW THE KILLER STRUCK AND ESCAPED SO QUICKLY AND SILENTLY AND WITHOUT BEING SEEN...

EACH DECLARED THAT SHE HAD BEEN WAKEFUL THE ENTIRE NIGHT BUT HAD HEARD NO CRY OR SOUND OF STRUGGLE.

ESPECIALLY SINCE, DUE TO THE EXTREMITY OF THE CRIME, HE MUST HAVE BEEN SOAKED IN BLOOD!

HOWEVER, BECAUSE NO SPURTING OR SPATTERING OF BLOOD WAS EVIDENT AT THE MURDER SCENE, THE CORONER CONCLUDED THAT THE VICTIM'S THROAT WAS CUT AS SHE LAY ON HER BACK... LEAVING THE KILLER RELATIVELY STAIN-FREE.

IN ANY CASE, IT SEEMS THAT BLOOD-COVERED HANDS AND CLOTHING ARE NOT UNUSUAL IN THIS DISTRICT OF SLAUGHTER-YARDS AND MEAT-PACKING HOUSES...

AND SO THE MURDERER MOST LIKELY EMERGED UNOBTRUSIVELY FROM HIS GRISLY WORK AND CALMLY JOINED THE EARLY MORNING TRAFFIC ALONG WHITECHAPEL ROAD.

SATURDAY 8 SEPTEMBER

THE VICTIM OF ANOTHER VIOLENT MURDER AND MUTILATION WAS DISCOVERED THIS MORNING IN BACK OF A LODGING-HOUSE AT 29 HANBURY STREET IN SPITALFIELDS. (NO MORE THAN ONE-HALF MILE FROM LAST WEEK'S TRAGEDY ON BUCK'S ROW).

AT ABOUT 6:00 AM, A LODGER NAMED DAVIS SOUGHT TO ENTER THE REAR YARD — WHICH IS OFTEN USED, I AM TOLD, BY THE LOCAL PROSTITUTES FOR THEIR WORK.

HE WAS HORRIFIED BY WHAT HE ENCOUNTERED: THE CORPSE OF A WOMAN, LYING FACE-UP AT THE FOOT OF THE STEPS!

HE THEN RAN SCREAMING INTO THE STREET, STARTLING THE NEIGHBOURHOOD...

THE RESULT BEING THAT A LARGE AND UNRULY CROWD HAD GATHERED BEFORE THE POLICE COULD BE SUMMONED.

AT LENGTH, INSPECTOR CHANDLER OF THE COMMERCIAL ST. STATION ARRIVED WITH HIS MEN TO SEAL-OFF THE BUILDING AND YARD.

DR. BAGSTER-PHILLIPS, THE DIVISIONAL SURGEON, MADE THE INITIAL EXAMINATION OF THE GRUESOME REMAINS.

AS WITH THE LAST VICTIM, THE WOMAN'S THROAT WAS CUT WITH TWO DEEP SLASHES — SO FORCEFUL THIS TIME THAT SHE WAS ALMOST BEHEADED! (A SCARF HAD BEEN PLACED ABOUT HER NECK AS IF TO HIDE THE INCISIONS.)

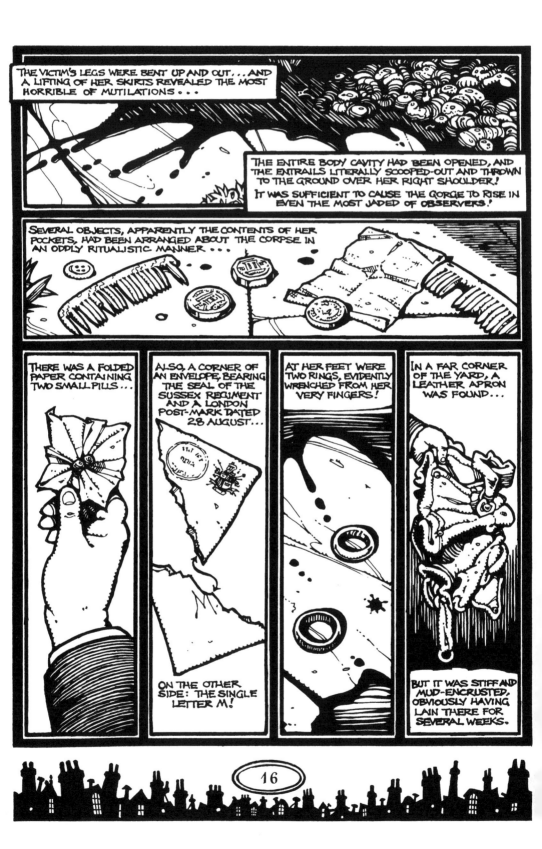

THE VICTIM'S LEGS WERE BENT UP AND OUT,... AND A LIFTING OF HER SKIRTS REVEALED THE MOST HORRIBLE OF MUTILATIONS...

THE ENTIRE BODY CAVITY HAD BEEN OPENED, AND THE ENTRAILS LITERALLY SCOOPED-OUT AND THROWN TO THE GROUND OVER HER RIGHT SHOULDER!

IT WAS SUFFICIENT TO CAUSE THE GORGE TO RISE IN EVEN THE MOST JADED OF OBSERVERS!

SEVERAL OBJECTS, APPARENTLY THE CONTENTS OF HER POCKETS, HAD BEEN ARRANGED ABOUT THE CORPSE IN AN ODDLY RITUALISTIC MANNER...

THERE WAS A FOLDED PAPER CONTAINING TWO SMALL PILLS...

ALSO, A CORNER OF AN ENVELOPE, BEARING THE SEAL OF THE SUSSEX REGIMENT AND A LONDON POST-MARK DATED 28 AUGUST...

ON THE OTHER SIDE: THE SINGLE LETTER M!

AT HER FEET WERE TWO RINGS, EVIDENTLY WRENCHED FROM HER VERY FINGERS!

IN A FAR CORNER OF THE YARD, A LEATHER APRON WAS FOUND...

BUT IT WAS STIFF AND MUD-ENCRUSTED, OBVIOUSLY HAVING LAIN THERE FOR SEVERAL WEEKS.

BAGSTER·PHILLIPS' POST·MORTEM THIS AFTERNOON CONFIRMED THE WORST VIOLATION IMAGINABLE: THE WOMAN'S SEXUAL ORGANS ARE MISSING ENTIRELY!!

INSPECTOR FREDERICK ABBERLINE OF GREAT SCOTLAND YARD — WHO KNOWS THE DISTRICT WELL — HAS BEEN ASSIGNED TO SUPERVISE THE INVESTIGATION, WHICH NOW INVOLVES HUNDREDS OF POLICEMEN.

THEIR TASK IS DIFFICULT ENOUGH IN THIS NEIGHBOURHOOD, WHOSE DENIZENS ARE NOT ORDINARILY INCLINED TO CO-OPERATE WITH THE CONSTABULARY.

TO MAKE MATTERS WORSE, ANGRY MOBS NOW STRIDE THE STREETS, IN A MOOD TO CAST BLAME IN ANY DIRECTION. TODAY, AS ALWAYS, THE JEWS MAKE A CONVENIENT TARGET.

THE JEWS DID IT!

DOWN WITH THE JEWS!

THE SEARCH FOR JOHN PIZER (KNOWN AS "LEATHER APRON") HAS BEEN INTENSIFIED, WITH SERGEANT WM. THICKE — A MOST ABLE DETECTIVE — IN COMPLETE CHARGE.

OTHER THAN THIS, THERE APPEAR TO BE NO FRUITFUL AVENUES TO FOLLOW.

MONDAY
10 SEPTEMBER

MR. BAXTER OPENED HIS INQUEST THIS MORNING OVER THE HANBURY STREET VICTIM: A SHORT, STOUT WOMAN NAMED ANNIE CHAPMAN (ALSO KNOWN AS ANNIE SIFFEY OR SIEVEY), AGED ABOUT 45 YEARS.

A FRIEND TO THE DECEASED, BY NAME OF AMELIA PALMER, FILLED IN THE STORY OF THE VICTIM'S UNHAPPY EXISTENCE:

LONG APART FROM HER HUSBAND AND CHILDREN, SHE HAD LIVED WITH DIFFERENT MEN ...

WHILE WORKING AS SEAMSTRESS OR FLOWER-SELLER ... BUT MORE OFTEN AS PROSTITUTE.

SHE WAS KNOWN TO LODGE LATELY AT 35 DORSET ST.

HER HEAVY DRINKING MADE HER THE SUBJECT OF BLACK SPELLS — AND GAINED HER THE NICK-NAME OF "DARK ANNIE."

DURING THESE PERIODS, SHE WOULD OFTEN INITIATE FURIOUS BRAWLS WITH CERTAIN OF THE OTHER WOMEN.

A MAN NAMED DONOVAN, DEPUTY AT THE DORSET STREET HOUSE, TESTIFIED THAT HE HAD TURNED THE DECEASED OUT AT 2:00 AM ON SATURDAY MORNING, FOR LACK OF "DOSS" MONEY.

COMMERCIAL STREET

HANBURY STREET

DORSET ST

FASHION STR

MRS. LONG, A LOCAL WIFE, SAID THAT SHE WAS WALKING TO MARKET ALONG HANBURY STREET AT 5:30 AM (A MERE HALF-HOUR BEFORE THE BODY WAS FOUND), WHEN SHE SAW THE DECEASED TALKING WITH A MAN:

A DARK, "FOREIGN-LOOKING" MAN OF ABOUT 40 YEARS...

WEARING A DARK COAT AND A DEER-STALKER HAT...

AND, OVER-ALL, OF A "SHABBY-GENTEEL" APPEARANCE.

PASSING THE COUPLE, SHE HEARD THE MAN ASK: "WILL YOU?" THE DECEASED REPLIED: "YES."

CAN THIS BE OUR FIRST REAL GLIMPSE OF THE KILLER?

ALSO THIS MORNING, THE ELUSIVE JOHN PIZER WAS TAKEN INTO CUSTODY AT LAST. SERGEANT THICKE DISCOVERED HIM HIDING AMONG RELATIONS ON MULBERRY STREET.

ANOTHER MAN, BY NAME OF PIGGOTT, HAS BEEN ARRESTED AT GRAVES-END. HIS HANDS AND CLOTHING WERE REPORTEDLY STAINED WITH BLOOD.

NO!

TUESDAY 11 SEPTEMBER
THE INQUEST RESUMED THIS MORNING WITH A MAN NAMED CADOSH, WHO LIVES IN THE HOUSE ADJACENT TO 29 HANBURY STREET.

AS HE LEFT THE HOUSE, AT ABOUT 5:20 AM, HE HEARD A CRY FROM THE NEXT YARD, AND THE SOUND OF SOMETHING FALLING AGAINST THE FENCE.

APPARENTLY, NOBODY ELSE WHO LIVES IN THE SURROUNDING HOUSES HEARD ANYTHING AT ALL.

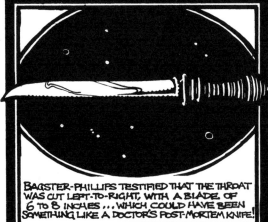

BAGSTER-PHILLIPS TESTIFIED THAT THE THROAT WAS CUT LEFT-TO-RIGHT, WITH A BLADE OF 6 TO 8 INCHES ... WHICH COULD HAVE BEEN SOMETHING LIKE A DOCTOR'S POST-MORTEM KNIFE!

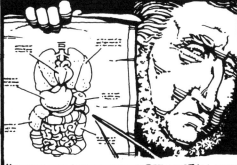

HE THEN DECLARED, TO THE SURPRISE OF ALL, THAT THE KILLER MUST BE A SURGEON, OR ELSE POSSESS ANATOMICAL KNOWLEDGE OF A SOPHISTICATED ORDER, TO HAVE LOCATED AND REMOVED THE SEXUAL ORGANS SO EASILY.

"THIS EVENING, THE NOTORIOUS PIZER WAS GIVEN HIS FREEDOM, HAVING BEEN ABLE TO VERIFY HIS WHEREABOUTS ON THE NIGHTS OF BOTH MURDERS. HE CONTINUES TO INSIST THAT HE HAS NEVER BEEN KNOWN AS "LEATHER APRON."

THE UNFORTUNATE PIGGOTT REMAINS IN CUSTODY AT GRAVES-END, BUT HIS DAZED DEMEANOR HAS CAUSED HIM TO BE ELIMINATED AS A SUSPECT.

TO-NIGHT, THE ENTIRE EAST END SHUDDERS UNDER THE HEAVY CLOUD OF FEAR.

THE POLICE-FORCE, I REALIZE, ARE TRULY DOING THEIR UTMOST... BUT WHAT, IN TRUTH, CAN BE DONE TO REPEL AN UNKNOWN ENEMY, WHO MOVES INVISIBLY AND STRIKES AT SEEMING RANDOM?

THE GOOD MERCHANTS AND TRADES-MEN OF WHITECHAPEL HAVE FORMED A VIGILANCE COMMITTEE FOR SELF-PROTECTION. IT IS HEADED BY MR. GEO. LUSK OF MILE-END ROAD.

ALREADY, THEY HAVE APPEALED TO THE GOVERNMENT FOR BETTER STREET-LIGHTING AND MORE FREQUENT POLICE PATROLS.

WEDNESDAY 26 SEPTEMBER

MR. BAXTER TODAY SUMMED UP THE EVIDENCE IN THE DEATHS OF ANNIE CHAPMAN AND "POLLY" NICHOLS WITH SOME ASTONISHING CONCLUSIONS.

HE SEEKS TO LINK THESE TWO MURDERS WITH THOSE EARLIER THIS YEAR OF MARTHA TABRAM AND EMMA SMITH TO FORM A SERIES OF CRIMES OF REMARKABLE SIMILARITY...

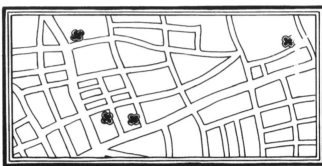

- ◉ ALL FOUR MURDERS WERE COMMITTED AFTER MID-NIGHT, OUT-OF-DOORS, CLOSE TO PUBLIC THOROUGHFARES
- ◉ ALL WITHIN ONE-HALF MILE OF ONE ANOTHER.
- ◉ THE VICTIMS WERE WOMEN OF MIDDLE-AGE AND INTEMPERATE HABITS, WITH NO FIXED ADDRESS...
- ◉ ALL OF THEM MURDERED BY KNIFE, FROM NO APPARENT MOTIVE, AFTER WHICH THE KILLER VANISHED.

FURTHER, HE ASKS US TO CONSIDER THAT THE KILLER IS NOT A LOCAL BUTCHER OR COMMON LABOURER...

BUT A SKILLED PERSON FROM THE UPPER OR PROFESSIONAL CLASSES, "SLUMMING" IN THE DISTRICT...

A MAN WHO KNOWS HUMAN ANATOMY AND WIELDS THE BLADE WITH A PRACTISED ECONOMY!

MR. BAXTER THEN OFFERED A SURPRISING THEORY AS TO MOTIVATION:

THE WOMEN WERE KILLED IN ORDER TO OBTAIN CERTAIN INTERNAL ORGANS...

A LUCRATIVE MARKET FOR WHICH IS KNOWN TO EXIST AMONG UNSCRUPULOUS DOCTORS AND MEDICAL SCHOOLS.

AN AMERICAN FORENSIC JOURNAL HAS REPORTEDLY OFFERED CASH PAYMENT FOR GENUINE BODY PARTS!

THE SCALPEL

I FIND I DO NOT COMPLETELY AGREE WITH THIS THEORY, ALTHOUGH IT HAS ITS INTERESTING POINTS.

SUNDAY 30 SEPTEMBER
TWO MORE MURDERS OF SHOCKING SEVERITY WERE COMMITTED THIS MORNING, ASSURING EVERYBODY THAT THE PHANTOM KILLER HAS NOT YET COMPLETED HIS WORK.

A STEADY RAIN WAS FALLING AT 1:00 A.M., WHEN MR. LOUIS DIEMSCHUTZ PULLED HIS CART INTO A NARROW COURT OFF O' BERNER STREET IN WHITECHAPEL.

HE FOUND HIS WAY BLOCKED BY A DARK FORM ON THE GROUND.

A WOMAN ON HER BACK... WAS SHE DEAD OR MERELY DRUNKEN?

MEN ARRIVED FROM DOWN THE COURT: THEIR LAMPS REVEALED HER SLASHED THROAT... AND THE BLOOD COLLECTED AROUND HER.

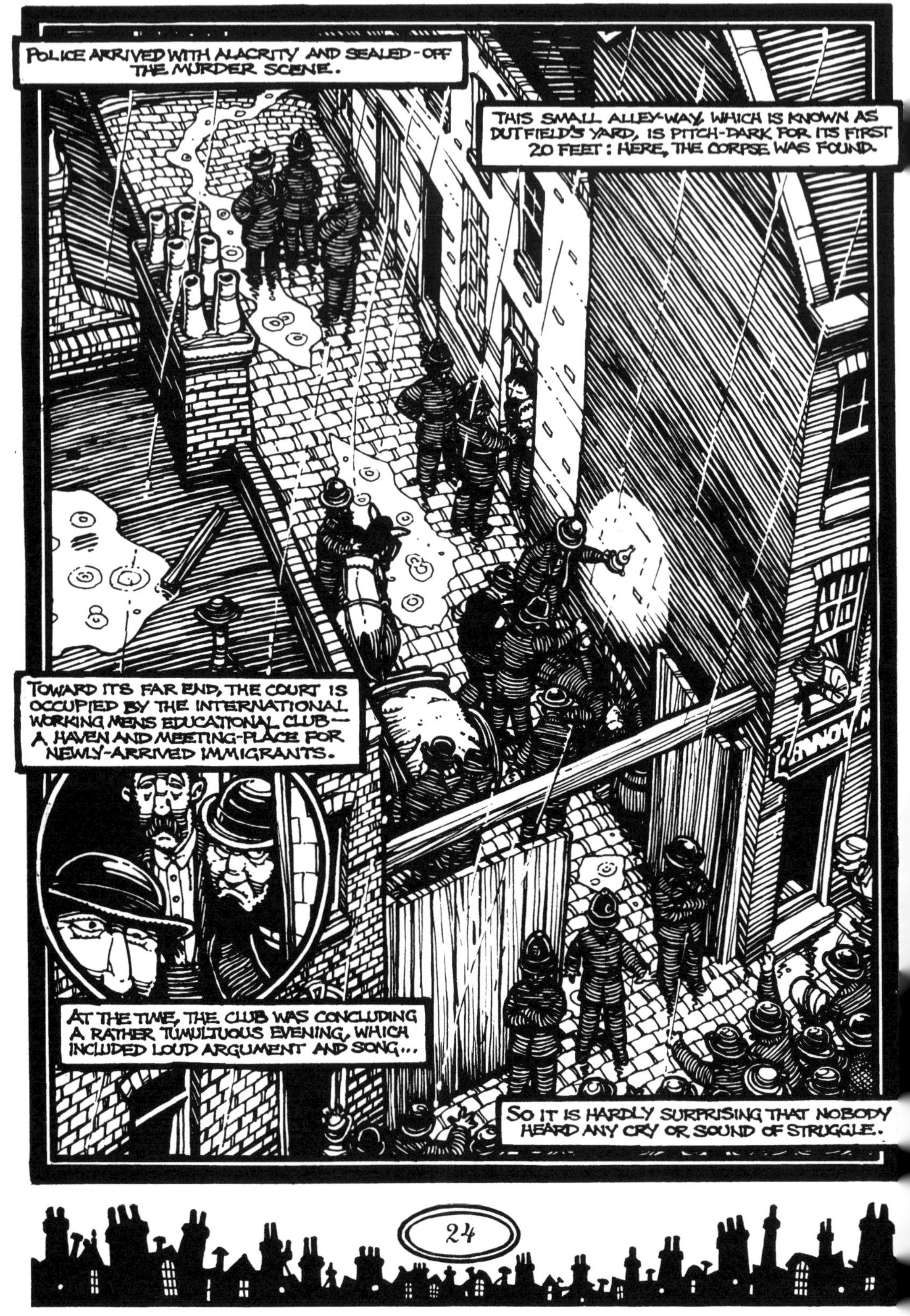
POLICE ARRIVED WITH ALACRITY AND SEALED-OFF THE MURDER SCENE.
THIS SMALL ALLEY-WAY, WHICH IS KNOWN AS DUTFIELD'S YARD, IS PITCH-DARK FOR ITS FIRST 20 FEET: HERE, THE CORPSE WAS FOUND.
TOWARD ITS FAR END, THE COURT IS OCCUPIED BY THE INTERNATIONAL WORKING MENS EDUCATIONAL CLUB— A HAVEN AND MEETING-PLACE FOR NEWLY-ARRIVED IMMIGRANTS.
AT THE TIME, THE CLUB WAS CONCLUDING A RATHER TUMULTUOUS EVENING, WHICH INCLUDED LOUD ARGUMENT AND SONG...
SO IT IS HARDLY SURPRISING THAT NOBODY HEARD ANY CRY OR SOUND OF STRUGGLE.

DR. BLACKWELL, A PHYSICIAN OF THE NEIGHBOURHOOD WAS FIRST TO EXAMINE THE REMAINS... JOINED SHORTLY BY BAGSTER-PHILLIPS.

THE BODY WAS STILL WARM... WITH A SINGLE SLASH TO THE THROAT.

THEY FOUND NO OTHER MUTILATIONS: COULD IT BE THE KILLER WAS INTERRUPTED WHEN HE HAD BARELY BEGUN?

PERHAPS THE CART ENTERING THE ALLEY-WAY DIVERTED HIM FROM HIS BUSINESS...

AND HE ESCAPED ROUND THE REAR OF IT.

THE POLICE, FOR THEIR PART, QUESTIONED THE MEMBERS OF THE WORKING MEN'S CLUB... TO THE EXTENT OF SEARCHING THEIR INDIVIDUAL HOMES!

THE PUBLIC OPINION IS AFLAME AGAINST FOREIGNERS! WHAT IS THERE ABOUT OUR NATIONAL CHARACTER THAT REFUSES TO IMAGINE AN ENGLISHMAN RESPONSIBLE FOR THESE OUTRAGES?

IN THE MEAN-TIME, NO MORE THAN A TEN-MINUTE WALK DISTANT, A SECOND BODY WAS FOUND!

AT 1:45, A CONSTABLE NAMED WATKINS ENTERED MITRE SQUARE, ALDGATE, WHICH IS OVER THE BOUNDARY FROM WHITECHAPEL INTO THE CITY OF LONDON.

HE HAD WALKED THROUGH THE SQUARE JUST 15 MINUTES EARLIER. AT THAT TIME, ALL HAD BEEN QUIET.

THIS TIME, AS HE ROUNDED THE CORNER, HE IMMEDIATELY SAW THE BODY OF A WOMAN ON HER BACK . . .

RIPPED OPEN, "LIKE A PIG IN THE MARKET," AS HE COLORFULLY PUT IT.

MITRE SQUARE IS SURROUNDED ON TWO SIDES BY THE WARE-HOUSES OF KEARLEY AND TONGE. THE OTHER SIDES ARE FRONTED BY OLD RESIDENCES, MANY OF THEM LYING EMPTY.

THE PASSAGE IS APT TO BE HIGHLY-FREQUENTED, EVEN AT THAT HOUR. THE KILLER COULD HAVE BEEN INTERRUPTED AT ANY MOMENT...

HE APPEARS TO BECOME MORE DARING—OR DESPERATE—WITH EACH CRIME!

SIR HENRY SMITH, THE ASSISTANT CITY POLICE COMMISSIONER, ARRIVED TO OVER-SEE THE INVESTIGATION.

DR. FREDERICK BROWN, THE CITY POLICE SURGEON, APPEARED AT 2:00 AM, TO MAKE THE INITIAL EXAMINATION. DR. SEQUIRA, FROM A NEAR-BY SURGERY, WAS ALSO IN ATTENDANCE.

HER THROAT HAD BEEN OPENED WITH A SINGLE DEEP STROKE; THE FACE DISFIGURED BY SEVERAL SMALL CUTS AND NIPS ...

INCLUDING A DIAGONAL SLASH THAT SEVERED THE TIP OF THE NOSE AND A PIECE OF THE RIGHT EAR!

AND THEN THE WOMAN HAD BEEN RIPPED COMPLETELY UP THE MIDDLE ...

AND, AS WITH THE HANBURY STREET VICTIM, THE INTERNAL VISCERA HAD BEEN SCOOPED OUT AND THROWN DOWN OVER THE RIGHT SHOULDER!

BOTH DOCTORS WERE IN AGREEMENT THAT THE DISEMBOWELMENT WAS HURRIED, CRUDE AND ARTLESS.

AGAIN, THERE WAS NO SIGN OF STRUGGLE, AND NO SPEWING OR SPATTERING OF BLOOD. INSTEAD, IT SLOWLY COLLECTED BENEATH THE BODY.

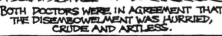

THROUGHOUT THE EARLY MORNING HOURS, OFFICERS OF THE CITY AND METROPOLITAN FORCES SWARMED OVER THE EAST END.

IT APPEARED AS IF THE KILLER HAD ESCAPED BACK INTO WHITECHAPEL.

ONE POLICEMAN CLAIMED TO HAVE FOUND BLOOD-STAINED WATER IN A BASIN ON DORSET STREET.

AT 4:00 AM, CONSTABLE ALFRED LONG EXAMINED THE ENTRANCE-WAY TO A BLOCK OF FLATS ON GOULSTON ST.

ON THE FLOOR WITHIN, HE FOUND A PIECE OF CLOTH FRESHLY SMEARED WITH BLOOD... AS IF USED TO WIPE A BLADE.!

ON A WALL NEAR-BY WAS A DISTURBING INSCRIPTION, SCRAWLED IN CHALK:

THE JUWES ARE NOT THE MEN THAT WILL BE BLAMED FOR NOTHING

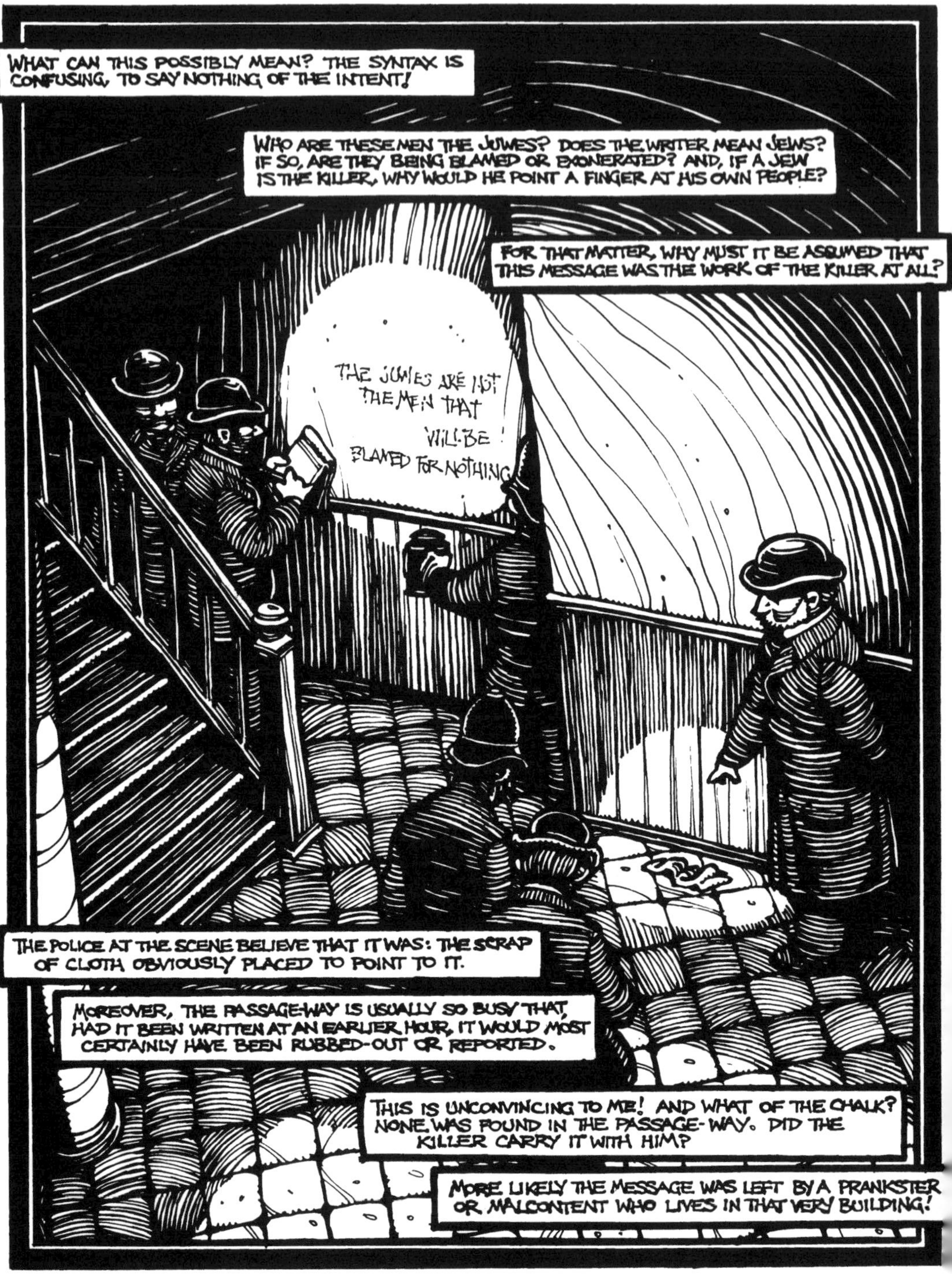
WHAT CAN THIS POSSIBLY MEAN? THE SYNTAX IS CONFUSING, TO SAY NOTHING OF THE INTENT!
WHO ARE THESE MEN THE JUWES? DOES THE WRITER MEAN JEWS? IF SO, ARE THEY BEING BLAMED OR EXONERATED? AND, IF A JEW IS THE KILLER, WHY WOULD HE POINT A FINGER AT HIS OWN PEOPLE?
FOR THAT MATTER, WHY MUST IT BE ASSUMED THAT THIS MESSAGE WAS THE WORK OF THE KILLER AT ALL?
THE JUWES ARE NOT THE MEN THAT WILL BE BLAMED FOR NOTHING
THE POLICE AT THE SCENE BELIEVE THAT IT WAS: THE SCRAP OF CLOTH OBVIOUSLY PLACED TO POINT TO IT.
MOREOVER, THE PASSAGE-WAY IS USUALLY SO BUSY THAT, HAD IT BEEN WRITTEN AT AN EARLIER HOUR, IT WOULD MOST CERTAINLY HAVE BEEN RUBBED-OUT OR REPORTED.
THIS IS UNCONVINCING TO ME! AND WHAT OF THE CHALK? NONE WAS FOUND IN THE PASSAGE-WAY. DID THE KILLER CARRY IT WITH HIM?
MORE LIKELY THE MESSAGE WAS LEFT BY A PRANKSTER OR MALCONTENT WHO LIVES IN THAT VERY BUILDING!

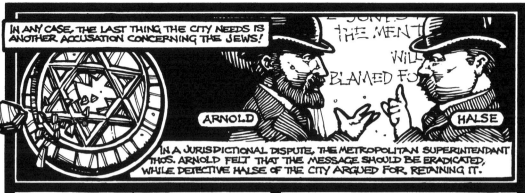

IN ANY CASE, THE LAST THING THE CITY NEEDS IS ANOTHER ACCUSATION CONCERNING THE JEWS!

ARNOLD

HALSE

IN A JURISDICTIONAL DISPUTE, THE METROPOLITAN SUPERINTENDANT THOS. ARNOLD FELT THAT THE MESSAGE SHOULD BE ERADICATED, WHILE DETECTIVE HALSE OF THE CITY ARGUED FOR RETAINING IT.

THE ARGUEMENT WAS SETTLED WHEN SIR CHAS. WARREN, THE METROPOLITAN POLICE COMMISSIONER ARRIVED AT ABOUT 5:30 AM

HE WAS ADAMANT IN HIS CONVICTION THAT THE INSCRIPTION SHOULD NOT ENDURE.

DESPITE VIGOUROUS OPPOSITION, HE REFUSED EVEN TO WAIT UNTIL DAYBREAK, WHEN A PHOTOGRAPHER COULD RECORD IT ...

AND, IN AN INEXCUSABLE BREACH OF INVESTIGATIVE PROCEDURE, PERSONALLY WIPED THE WRITING FROM THE WALL!

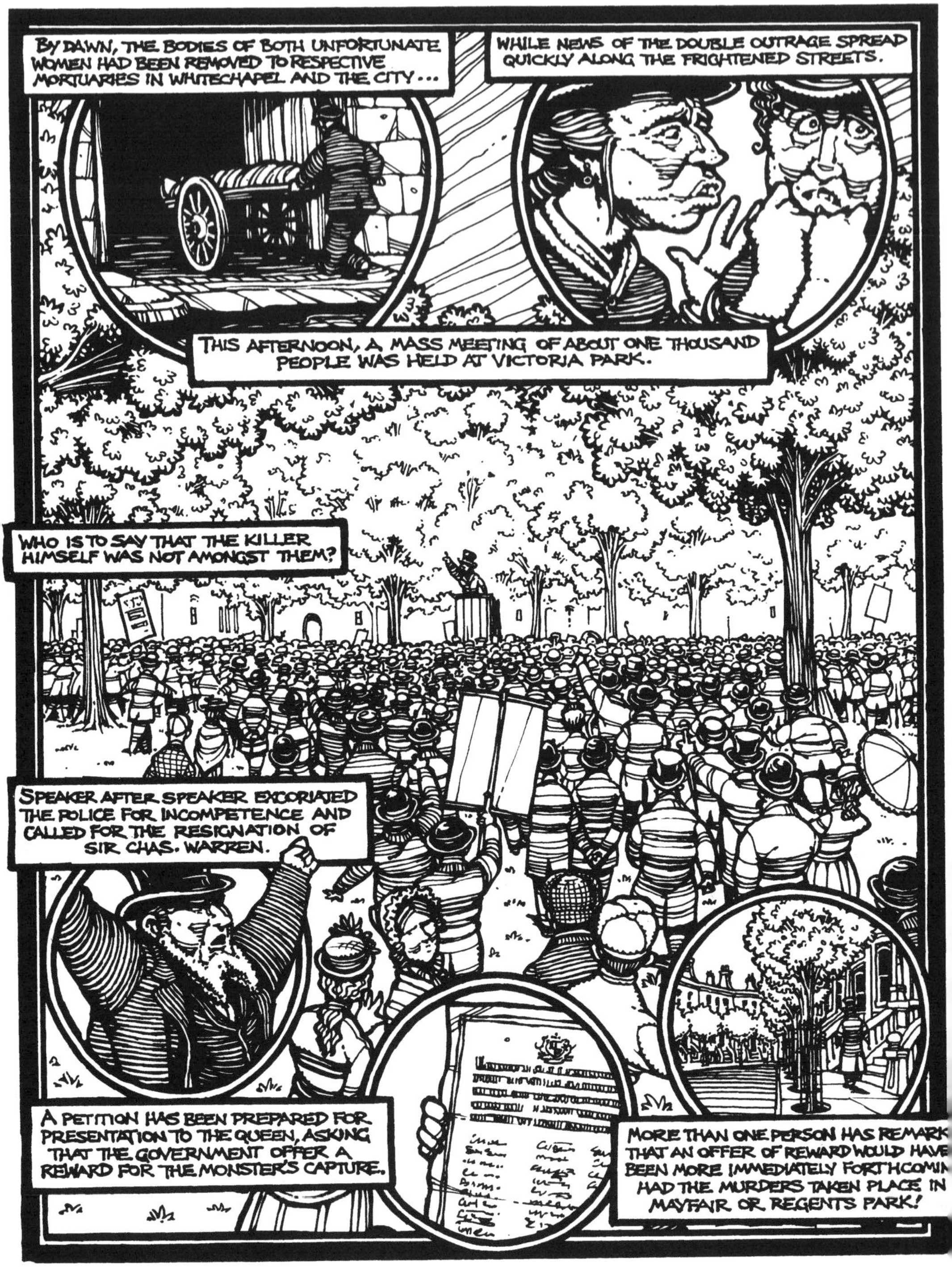
BY DAWN, THE BODIES OF BOTH UNFORTUNATE WOMEN HAD BEEN REMOVED TO RESPECTIVE MORTUARIES IN WHITECHAPEL AND THE CITY...
WHILE NEWS OF THE DOUBLE OUTRAGE SPREAD QUICKLY ALONG THE FRIGHTENED STREETS.
THIS AFTERNOON, A MASS MEETING OF ABOUT ONE THOUSAND PEOPLE WAS HELD AT VICTORIA PARK.
WHO IS TO SAY THAT THE KILLER HIMSELF WAS NOT AMONGST THEM?
SPEAKER AFTER SPEAKER EXCORIATED THE POLICE FOR INCOMPETENCE AND CALLED FOR THE RESIGNATION OF SIR CHAS. WARREN.
A PETITION HAS BEEN PREPARED FOR PRESENTATION TO THE QUEEN, ASKING THAT THE GOVERNMENT OFFER A REWARD FOR THE MONSTER'S CAPTURE.
MORE THAN ONE PERSON HAS REMARK THAT AN OFFER OF REWARD WOULD HAVE BEEN MORE IMMEDIATELY FORTHCOMIN HAD THE MURDERS TAKEN PLACE IN MAYFAIR OR REGENTS PARK!

ALSO THIS AFTERNOON, THE DOCTORS BROWN AND SEQUIRA PERFORMED THE POST-MORTEM UPON THE VICTIM FOUND IN MITRE SQUARE.

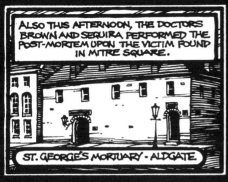

ST. GEORGE'S MORTUARY · ALDGATE.

A SISTER TO THE WOMAN IDENTIFIED HER AS CATHERINE, OR KATE, EDDOWES (ALSO CALLED KATE KELLY) AGED 43 YEARS.

THE DOCTORS FOUND THAT THE UTERUS AND THE LEFT KIDNEY WERE MISSING ENTIRELY!

IT WAS CONFIRMED THAT THE SCRAP OF CLOTH FOUND ON GOULSTON ST. MATCHES THE VICTIM'S SKIRT.

POLICE ALSO ADMITTED (TO THEIR GREAT EMBARRASSMENT) THAT UNTIL SHORTLY BEFORE HER DEATH SHE WAS IN THEIR CUSTODY AT THE BISHOPSGATE STATION!

INTO HER POCKETS WERE STUFFED THE WHOLE OF HER WORLDLY POSSESSIONS,

MONDAY 1 OCTOBER

NEWS OF THE MURDERS WAS PUBLISHED THIS MORNING THROUGH-OUT THE NATION. LONDON CAN TALK OF NOTHING ELSE.

EAST-END HORRORS
DOUBLE TRAGEDY
WEAPON FOUND
The Daily Mail

THE BERNER STREET VICTIM WAS IDENTIFIED BY SEVERAL ACQUAINTANCES AS ELIZABETH STRIDE, A SWEDISH WOMAN OF ABOUT 45 YEARS... KNOWN ABOUT THE DISTRICT AS "LONG LIZ."

BAGSTER-PHILLIPS, UNDER GREAT PROTEST, ONCE AGAIN PERFORMED THE POST-MORTEM AT THE DANK AND ILL-EQUIPPED WORK-HOUSE MORTUARY IN WHITECHAPEL.

APART FROM THE DEEP SLASH TO THE THROAT, HE AND DR. BLACKWELL COULD CONFIRM NO VIOLATIONS WHAT-EVER.

THE GENERAL FEELING IS STILL THAT THE KILLER WAS INTERRUPTED. BUT PERHAPS THIS WAS THE WORK OF AN IMITATOR.... OR ELSE THE RESULT OF A TOTALLY UNRELATED DISPUTE!

A BLOOD-SMEARED KNIFE, FOUND SUNDAY MORNING ON WHITECHAPEL ROAD, IS SEEN BY INVESTIGATORS AS "POSSIBLY" THE MURDER WEAPON.

MR. BAXTER OPENED THE INQUEST THIS AFTER-NOON AT THE VESTRY HALL ON CABLE STREET.

TESTIMONY BY VARIOUS FRIENDS OF THE DECEASED ESTABLISHED THAT HER ACTUAL NAME IS GUSTAFDOTTIR, BORN NEAR GOTHEBORG, SWEDEN AND EMIGRATED TO LONDON IN 1866.

SHE MARRIED A MAN NAMED STRIDE, AND THEY PRODUCED TWO OFF-SPRING.

(SHE ALWAYS CLAIMED THAT HER HUSBAND AND CHILDREN HAD PERISHED IN THE WRECK OF THE "PRINCESS ALICE" IN 1878.)

FOR SEVERAL YEARS, SHE LIVED ON FASHION STREET WITH A DOCK-WORKER NAMED KIDNEY.

BUT SHE WOULD DRIFT AWAY FOR DAYS, IN THE GRIP OF ALCOHOL... SUPPORTING HERSELF BY PROSTITUTION.

OFTEN ARRESTED FOR DRUNKENNESS, SHE WOULD INSIST THAT SHE MERELY SUFFERED FROM "FITS."

SHE IS KNOWN TO HAVE LODGED RECENTLY IN A "DOSS" HOUSE AT 32 FLOWER AND DEAN ST.

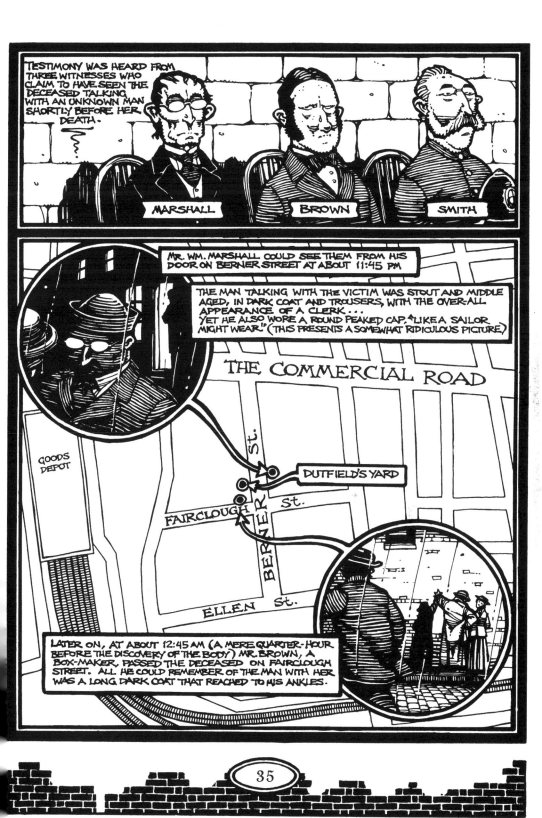

TESTIMONY WAS HEARD FROM THREE WITNESSES WHO CLAIM TO HAVE SEEN THE DECEASED TALKING WITH AN UNKNOWN MAN SHORTLY BEFORE HER DEATH.

MARSHALL

BROWN

SMITH

MR. WM. MARSHALL COULD SEE THEM FROM HIS DOOR ON BERNER STREET AT ABOUT 11:45 PM

THE MAN TALKING WITH THE VICTIM WAS STOUT AND MIDDLE AGED, IN DARK COAT AND TROUSERS, WITH THE OVER-ALL APPEARANCE OF A CLERK...
YET HE ALSO WORE A ROUND PEAKED CAP, "LIKE A SAILOR MIGHT WEAR." (THIS PRESENTS A SOMEWHAT RIDICULOUS PICTURE.)

THE COMMERCIAL ROAD

GOODS DEPOT

BERNER St.

DUTFIELD'S YARD

FAIRCLOUGH St.

ELLEN St.

LATER ON, AT ABOUT 12:45 AM (A MERE QUARTER-HOUR BEFORE THE DISCOVERY OF THE BODY) MR. BROWN, A BOX-MAKER, PASSED THE DECEASED ON FAIRCLOUGH STREET. ALL HE COULD REMEMBER OF THE MAN WITH HER WAS A LONG DARK COAT THAT REACHED TO HIS ANKLES.

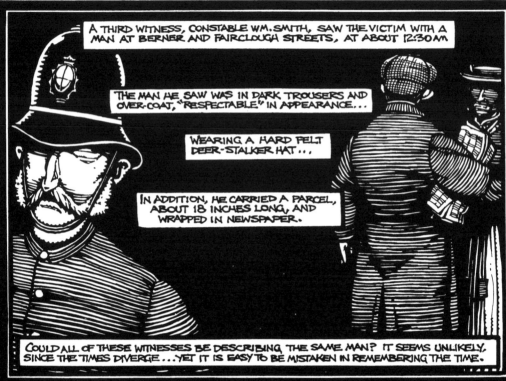

A THIRD WITNESS, CONSTABLE WM. SMITH, SAW THE VICTIM WITH A MAN AT BERNER AND FAIRCLOUGH STREETS, AT ABOUT 12:30 AM

THE MAN HE SAW WAS IN DARK TROUSERS AND OVER-COAT, "RESPECTABLE" IN APPEARANCE...

WEARING A HARD FELT DEER-STALKER HAT...,

IN ADDITION, HE CARRIED A PARCEL, ABOUT 18 INCHES LONG, AND WRAPPED IN NEWSPAPER.

COULD ALL OF THESE WITNESSES BE DESCRIBING THE SAME MAN? IT SEEMS UNLIKELY, SINCE THE TIMES DIVERGE... YET IT IS EASY TO BE MISTAKEN IN REMEMBERING THE TIME.

YET A FOURTH WITNESS, MR. ISRAEL SCHWARTZ, HAS BEEN INTERVIEWED BY THE POLICE, THOUGH NOT CALLED TO THE INQUEST.

HE RECALLS HAVING SEEN THE DECEASED ON BERNER STREET, WITH A MOUSTACHIOED MAN IN A DARK COAT, AND A ROUND PEAKED CAP.

THE MAN PUSHED HER TO THE GROUND. SHE SCREAMED AS HE DRAGGED HER INTO THE ALLEY-WAY.

INVESTIGATORS PLACE GREAT STOCK IN MR. SCHWARTZ'S ACCOUNT. YET WHY WAS HE NOT PRESENT AT THE INQUEST?

THE METROPOLITAN POLICE ANNOUNCED THIS AFTERNOON THE RECEIPT OF TWO REMARKABLE COMMUNICATIONS... FROM A PERSON CLAIMING TO BE THE KILLER!

BOTH WERE RECEIVED BY THE CENTRAL NEWS AGENCY. THE FIRST—PENNED IN RED INK—IS DATED LAST TUESDAY BUT WAS POSTED TWO DAYS LATER.

IT BEGINS: "DEAR BOSS."

"I AM DOWN ON WHORES AND I SHAN'T QUIT RIPPING THEM..."

"I LOVE MY WORK AND WANT TO START AGAIN..."

"THE NEXT JOB I DO, I SHALL CLIP THE LADY'S EARS OFF..."

"MY KNIFE IS NICE AND SHARP..."

HE EVEN EXPLAINS WHY HE COULD NOT WRITE THE MESSAGE IN HIS VICTIM'S BLOOD: "IT WENT THICK LIKE GLUE..."

HE CONCLUDES WITH A WISH OF "GOOD LUCK." AND SIGNS, "YOURS TRULY *Jack the Ripper*

THIS LETTER, LIKE HUNDREDS OF OTHERS RECEIVED, WAS DEEMED A HOAX... UNTIL THE ARRIVAL TODAY OF THE SECOND MESSAGE.

Dear Boss 23 *Sept* 1888

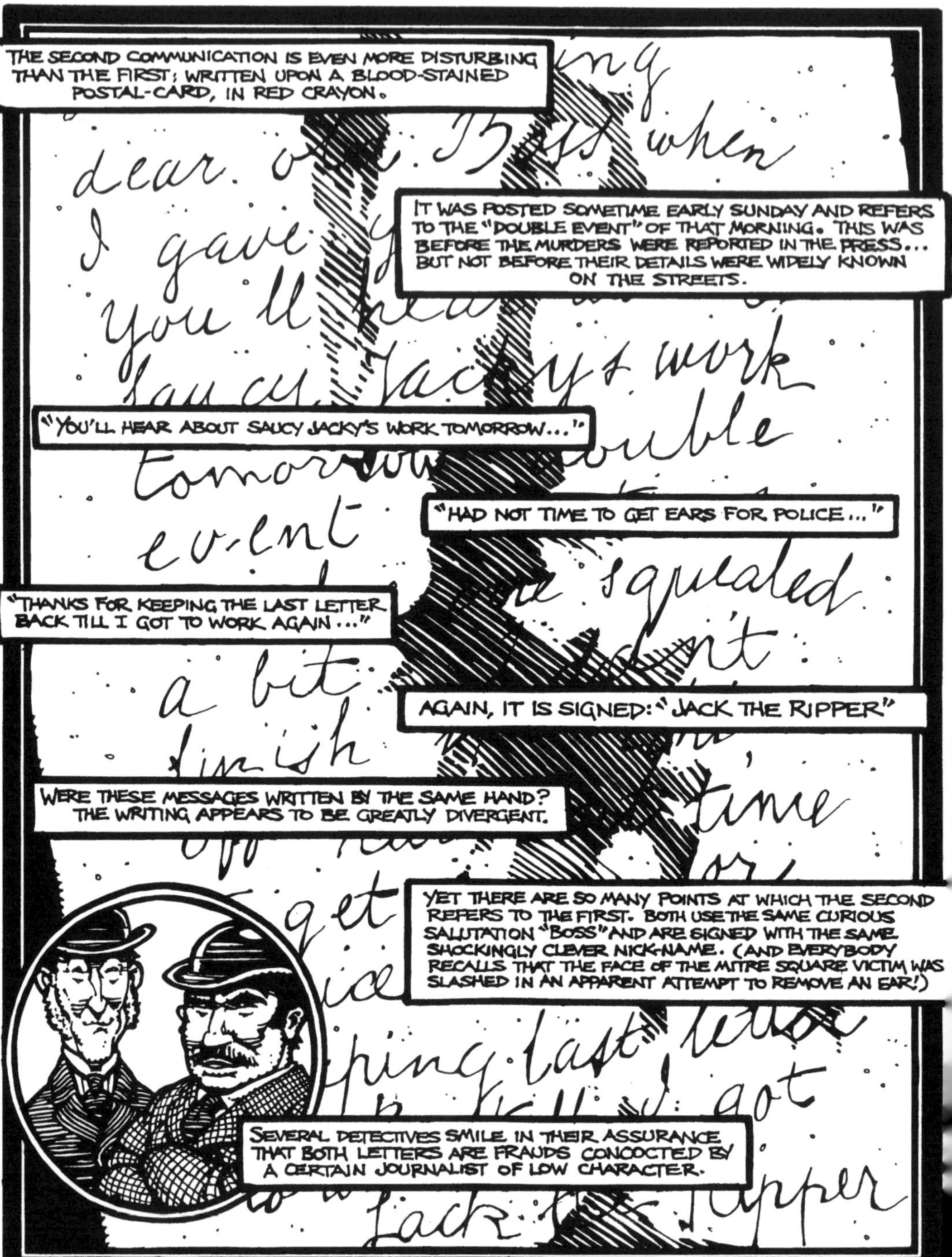
THE SECOND COMMUNICATION IS EVEN MORE DISTURBING THAN THE FIRST; WRITTEN UPON A BLOOD-STAINED POSTAL-CARD, IN RED CRAYON.
IT WAS POSTED SOMETIME EARLY SUNDAY AND REFERS TO THE "DOUBLE EVENT" OF THAT MORNING. THIS WAS BEFORE THE MURDERS WERE REPORTED IN THE PRESS... BUT NOT BEFORE THEIR DETAILS WERE WIDELY KNOWN ON THE STREETS.
"YOU'LL HEAR ABOUT SAUCY JACKY'S WORK TOMORROW..."
"HAD NOT TIME TO GET EARS FOR POLICE..."
"THANKS FOR KEEPING THE LAST LETTER BACK TILL I GOT TO WORK AGAIN..."
AGAIN, IT IS SIGNED: "JACK THE RIPPER"
WERE THESE MESSAGES WRITTEN BY THE SAME HAND? THE WRITING APPEARS TO BE GREATLY DIVERGENT.
YET THERE ARE SO MANY POINTS AT WHICH THE SECOND REFERS TO THE FIRST. BOTH USE THE SAME CURIOUS SALUTATION "BOSS" AND ARE SIGNED WITH THE SAME SHOCKINGLY CLEVER NICK-NAME. (AND EVERYBODY RECALLS THAT THE FACE OF THE MITRE SQUARE VICTIM WAS SLASHED IN AN APPARENT ATTEMPT TO REMOVE AN EAR!)
SEVERAL DETECTIVES SMILE IN THEIR ASSURANCE THAT BOTH LETTERS ARE FRAUDS CONCOCTED BY A CERTAIN JOURNALIST OF LOW CHARACTER.

THE LETTERS ARE APPARENTLY CONSIDERED AUTHENTIC ENOUGH TO REPRODUCE AND DISTRIBUTE ON HAND-BILLS THROUGH-OUT THE EAST END.

THE NOTED WRITER CONAN DOYLE HAS REMARKED UPON THE "AMERICANISMS" IN BOTH MESSAGES...

AND GOES SO FAR AS TO SUGGEST THAT POLICE LOOK FOR AN AMERICAN!

IN DUE COURSE, AN AMERICAN WAS ARRESTED THIS EVENING IN WHITECHAPEL.

SUPPOSEDLY, HE HAD ACCOSTED A WOMAN ON CABLE STREET AND THREATENED TO "RIP HER UP."

AT THE LEMAN STREET STATION, HE REPORTEDLY ASKED THE INSPECTOR IN CHARGE: "ARE YOU THE BOSS?"

BUT HE IS NEWLY-ARRIVED IN ENGLAND, AND IT SEEMS LIKELY HE WILL BE RELEASED BY MORNING.

THE PUBLIC MAY BE INCLINED TO SCORN INSPECTOR ABBERLINE AND HIS MEN FOR THEIR LACK OF SUCCESS THUS FAR...

INSP. NAIRN • SGT. PEARCE • SGT. THICKE • SGT. GODLEY • ABBERLINE • INSP. MOORE • INSP. REID • SGT. McCARTHY

BUT THEIR QUARRY CERTAINLY IS A PERSON WHO WORKS FROM IMPULSES DIVORCED FROM THOSE OF THE WORK-A-DAY THIEF AND CUT-THROAT.

THURSDAY 4 OCTOBER

THE CORONER'S INQUEST UPON CATHERINE EDDOWES, THE MITRE SQUARE VICTIM, BEGAN THIS MORNING AT THE GOLDEN LANE MORTUARY...

UNDER MR. LANGHAM, CITY CORONER.

FRIENDS OF THE DECEASED RECOUNTED HER SAD (AND ALL-TOO-FAMILIAR) HISTORY: A HUSBAND AND THREE OFFSPRING LEFT BEHIND FOR A LIFE OF DRUNKENNESS AND INCREASING DISSOLUTION.

SHE HAD LIVED RECENTLY WITH A LABOURER NAMED KELLY ON FLOWER AND DEAN STREET. TOGETHER, THEY FOUND ODD JOBS IN THE MARKETS.

BUT SHE WOULD MORE OFTEN, WHEN IN NEED OF FUNDS, SEEK CLIENTELE ON THE STREETS.

AT ABOUT 8:30 LAST SATURDAY EVENING, SHE WAS FOUND PASSED-OUT ON THE PAVEMENT IN ALDGATE AND TAKEN TO THE BISHOPSGATE STATION.

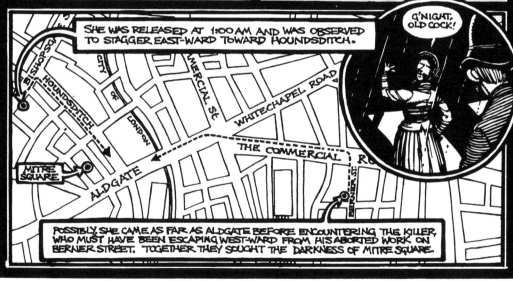

SHE WAS RELEASED AT 1:00 AM AND WAS OBSERVED TO STAGGER EAST-WARD TOWARD HOUNDSDITCH.

G'NIGHT, OLD COCK!

POSSIBLY, SHE CAME AS FAR AS ALDGATE BEFORE ENCOUNTERING THE KILLER, WHO MUST HAVE BEEN ESCAPING WEST-WARD FROM HIS ABORTED WORK ON BERNER STREET. TOGETHER THEY SOUGHT THE DARKNESS OF MITRE SQUARE.

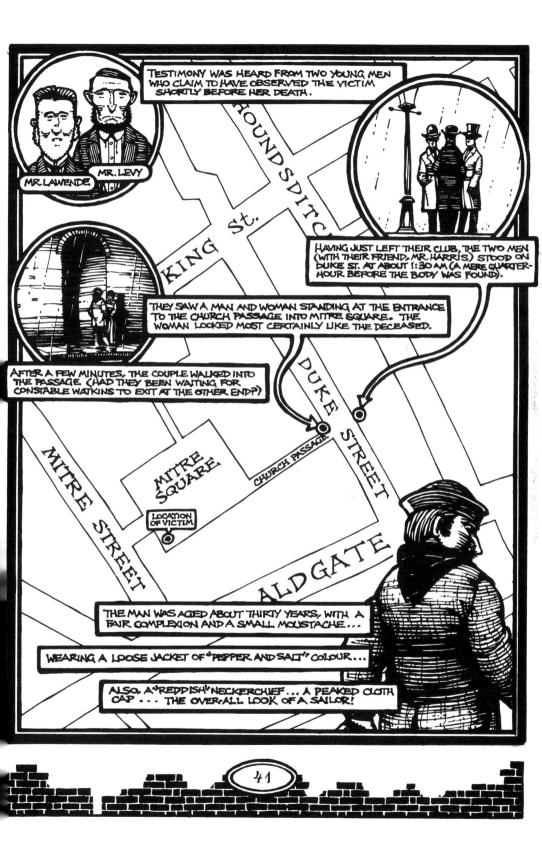

TESTIMONY WAS HEARD FROM TWO YOUNG MEN WHO CLAIM TO HAVE OBSERVED THE VICTIM SHORTLY BEFORE HER DEATH.

MR. LAWENDE   MR. LEVY

HAVING JUST LEFT THEIR CLUB, THE TWO MEN (WITH THEIR FRIEND, MR. HARRIS) STOOD ON DUKE ST. AT ABOUT 1:30 AM (A MERE QUARTER-HOUR BEFORE THE BODY WAS FOUND).

THEY SAW A MAN AND WOMAN STANDING AT THE ENTRANCE TO THE CHURCH PASSAGE INTO MITRE SQUARE. THE WOMAN LOOKED MOST CERTAINLY LIKE THE DECEASED.

AFTER A FEW MINUTES, THE COUPLE WALKED INTO THE PASSAGE. (HAD THEY BEEN WAITING FOR CONSTABLE WATKINS TO EXIT AT THE OTHER END?)

HOUNDSDITCH

KING St.

DUKE STREET

CHURCH PASSAGE

MITRE SQUARE

LOCATION OF VICTIM

MITRE STREET

ALDGATE

THE MAN WAS AGED ABOUT THIRTY YEARS, WITH A FAIR COMPLEXION AND A SMALL MOUSTACHE...

WEARING A LOOSE JACKET OF "PEPPER AND SALT" COLOUR...

ALSO, A "REDDISH" NECKERCHIEF... A PEAKED CLOTH CAP... THE OVER-ALL LOOK OF A SAILOR!

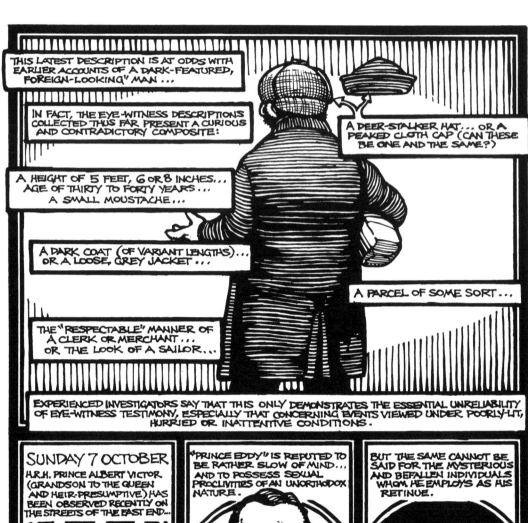

THIS LATEST DESCRIPTION IS AT ODDS WITH EARLIER ACCOUNTS OF A "DARK-FEATURED, FOREIGN-LOOKING" MAN...

IN FACT, THE EYE-WITNESS DESCRIPTIONS COLLECTED THUS FAR PRESENT A CURIOUS AND CONTRADICTORY COMPOSITE:

A DEER-STALKER HAT... OR A PEAKED CLOTH CAP (CAN THESE BE ONE AND THE SAME?)

A HEIGHT OF 5 FEET, 6 OR 8 INCHES... AGE OF THIRTY TO FORTY YEARS... A SMALL MOUSTACHE...

A DARK COAT (OF VARIANT LENGTHS)... OR A LOOSE, GREY JACKET...

A PARCEL OF SOME SORT...

THE "RESPECTABLE" MANNER OF A CLERK OR MERCHANT... OR THE LOOK OF A SAILOR...

EXPERIENCED INVESTIGATORS SAY THAT THIS ONLY DEMONSTRATES THE ESSENTIAL UNRELIABILITY OF EYE-WITNESS TESTIMONY, ESPECIALLY THAT CONCERNING EVENTS VIEWED UNDER POORLY-LIT, HURRIED OR INATTENTIVE CONDITIONS.

SUNDAY 7 OCTOBER

H.R.H. PRINCE ALBERT VICTOR (GRANDSON TO THE QUEEN AND HEIR-PRESUMPTIVE) HAS BEEN OBSERVED RECENTLY ON THE STREETS OF THE EAST END...

MOST OFTEN IN THE VICINITY OF A CERTAIN "HOUSE" ON CLEVELAND STREET!

"PRINCE EDDY" IS REPUTED TO BE RATHER SLOW OF MIND... AND TO POSSESS SEXUAL PROCLIVITIES OF AN UNORTHODOX NATURE.

NO-BODY AS YET SPECULATES THAT HE HAS ANY CONNEXION TO THESE CRIMES...

BUT THE SAME CANNOT BE SAID FOR THE MYSTERIOUS AND BEFALLEN INDIVIDUALS WHOM HE EMPLOYS AS HIS RETINUE.

I AM CERTAIN THAT WE SHALL HEAR MORE OF THIS AS TIME PROGRESSES.

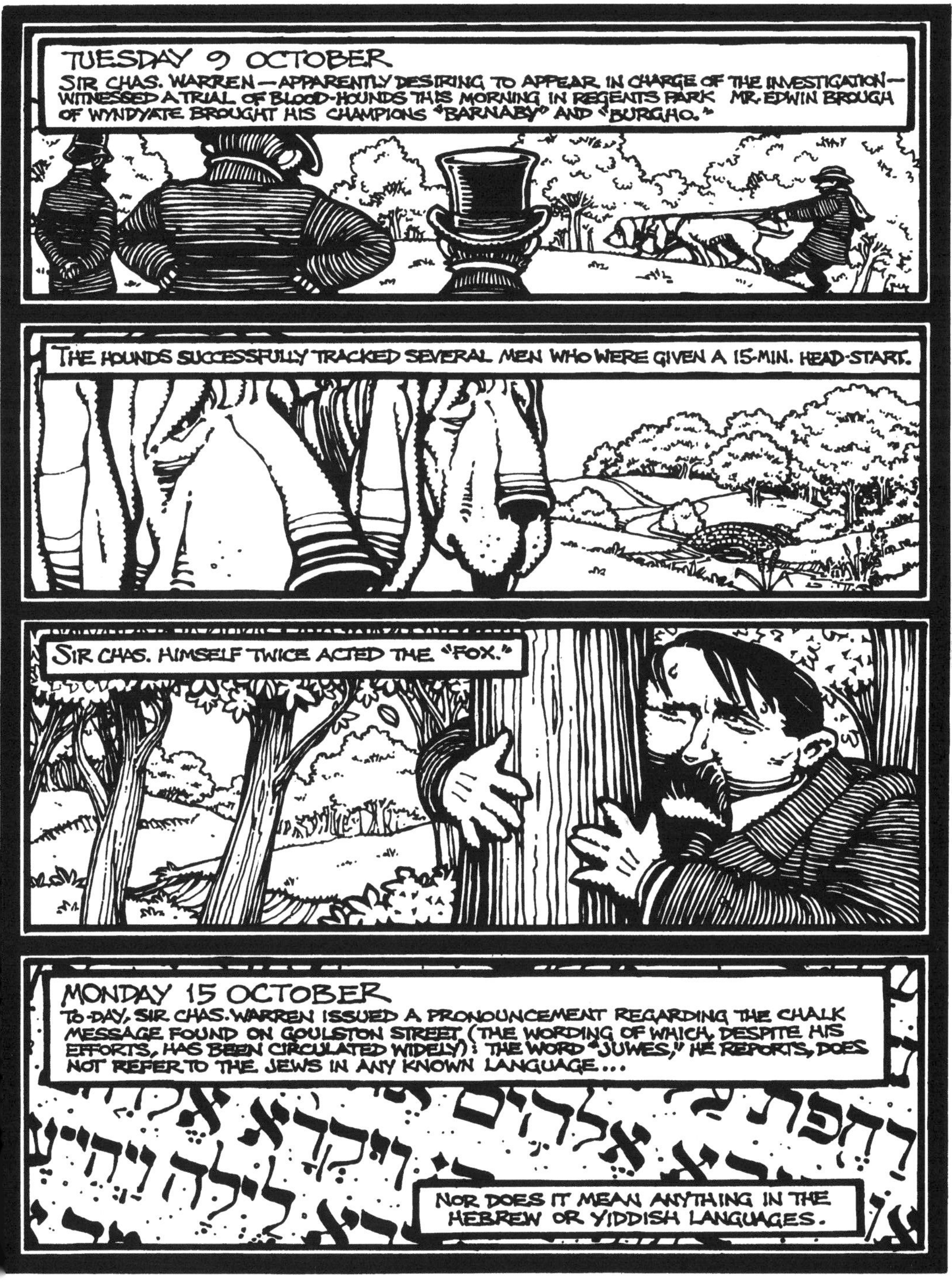
TUESDAY 9 OCTOBER
SIR CHAS. WARREN—APPARENTLY DESIRING TO APPEAR IN CHARGE OF THE INVESTIGATION—WITNESSED A TRIAL OF BLOOD-HOUNDS THIS MORNING IN REGENTS PARK. MR. EDWIN BROUGH OF WYNDYATE BROUGHT HIS CHAMPIONS "BARNABY" AND "BURGHO."
THE HOUNDS SUCCESSFULLY TRACKED SEVERAL MEN WHO WERE GIVEN A 15-MIN. HEAD-START.
SIR CHAS. HIMSELF TWICE ACTED THE "FOX."
MONDAY 15 OCTOBER
TO-DAY, SIR CHAS. WARREN ISSUED A PRONOUNCEMENT REGARDING THE CHALK MESSAGE FOUND ON GOULSTON STREET (THE WORDING OF WHICH, DESPITE HIS EFFORTS, HAS BEEN CIRCULATED WIDELY): THE WORD "JUWES," HE REPORTS, DOES NOT REFER TO THE JEWS IN ANY KNOWN LANGUAGE...
NOR DOES IT MEAN ANYTHING IN THE HEBREW OR YIDDISH LANGUAGES.

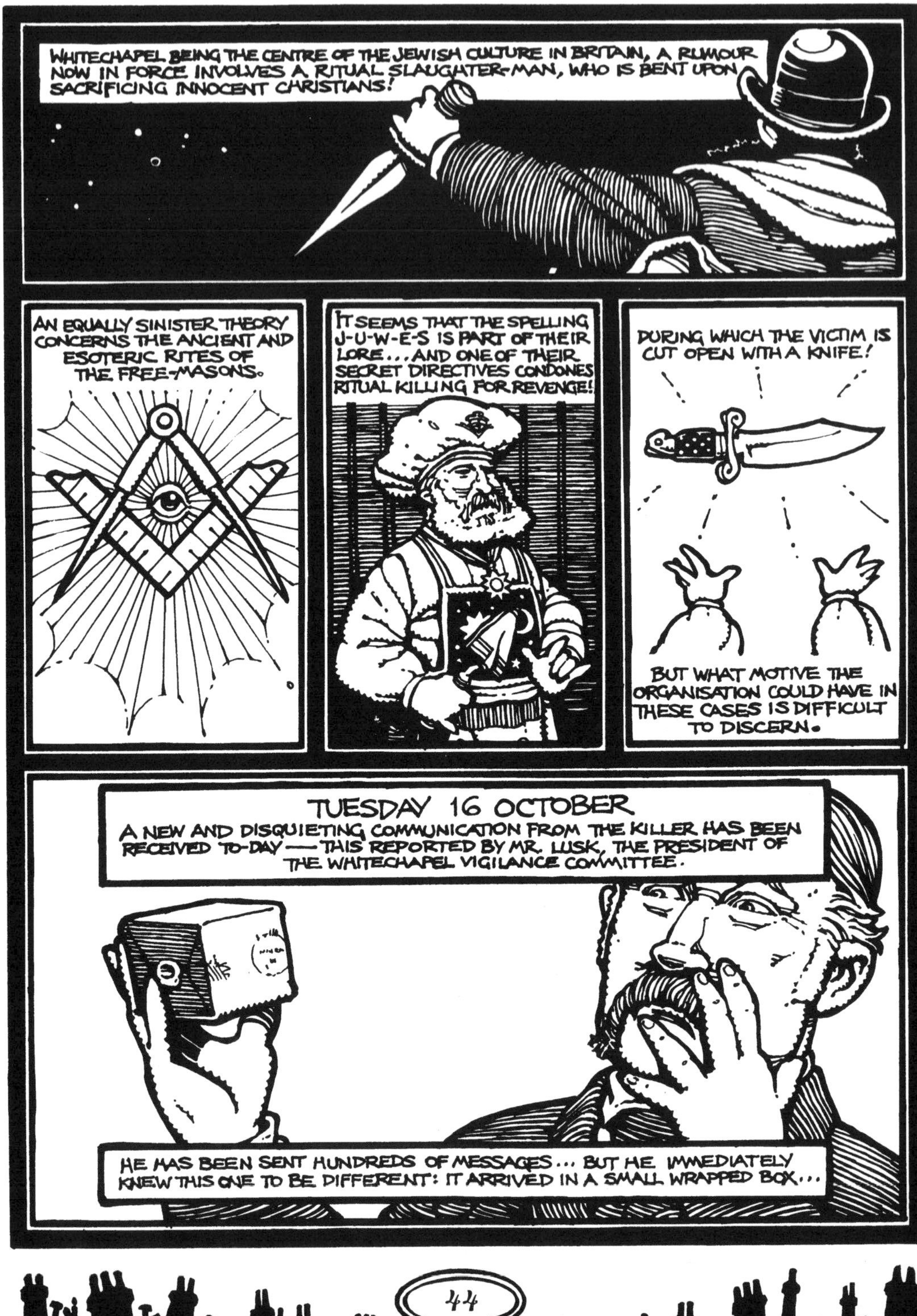

WHITECHAPEL BEING THE CENTRE OF THE JEWISH CULTURE IN BRITAIN, A RUMOUR NOW IN FORCE INVOLVES A RITUAL SLAUGHTER-MAN, WHO IS BENT UPON SACRIFICING INNOCENT CHRISTIANS!
AN EQUALLY SINISTER THEORY CONCERNS THE ANCIENT AND ESOTERIC RITES OF THE FREE-MASONS.
IT SEEMS THAT THE SPELLING J-U-W-E-S IS PART OF THEIR LORE... AND ONE OF THEIR SECRET DIRECTIVES CONDONES RITUAL KILLING FOR REVENGE!
DURING WHICH THE VICTIM IS CUT OPEN WITH A KNIFE!
BUT WHAT MOTIVE THE ORGANISATION COULD HAVE IN THESE CASES IS DIFFICULT TO DISCERN.
TUESDAY 16 OCTOBER
A NEW AND DISQUIETING COMMUNICATION FROM THE KILLER HAS BEEN RECEIVED TO-DAY — THIS REPORTED BY MR. LUSK, THE PRESIDENT OF THE WHITECHAPEL VIGILANCE COMMITTEE.
HE HAS BEEN SENT HUNDREDS OF MESSAGES... BUT HE IMMEDIATELY KNEW THIS ONE TO BE DIFFERENT: IT ARRIVED IN A SMALL WRAPPED BOX...

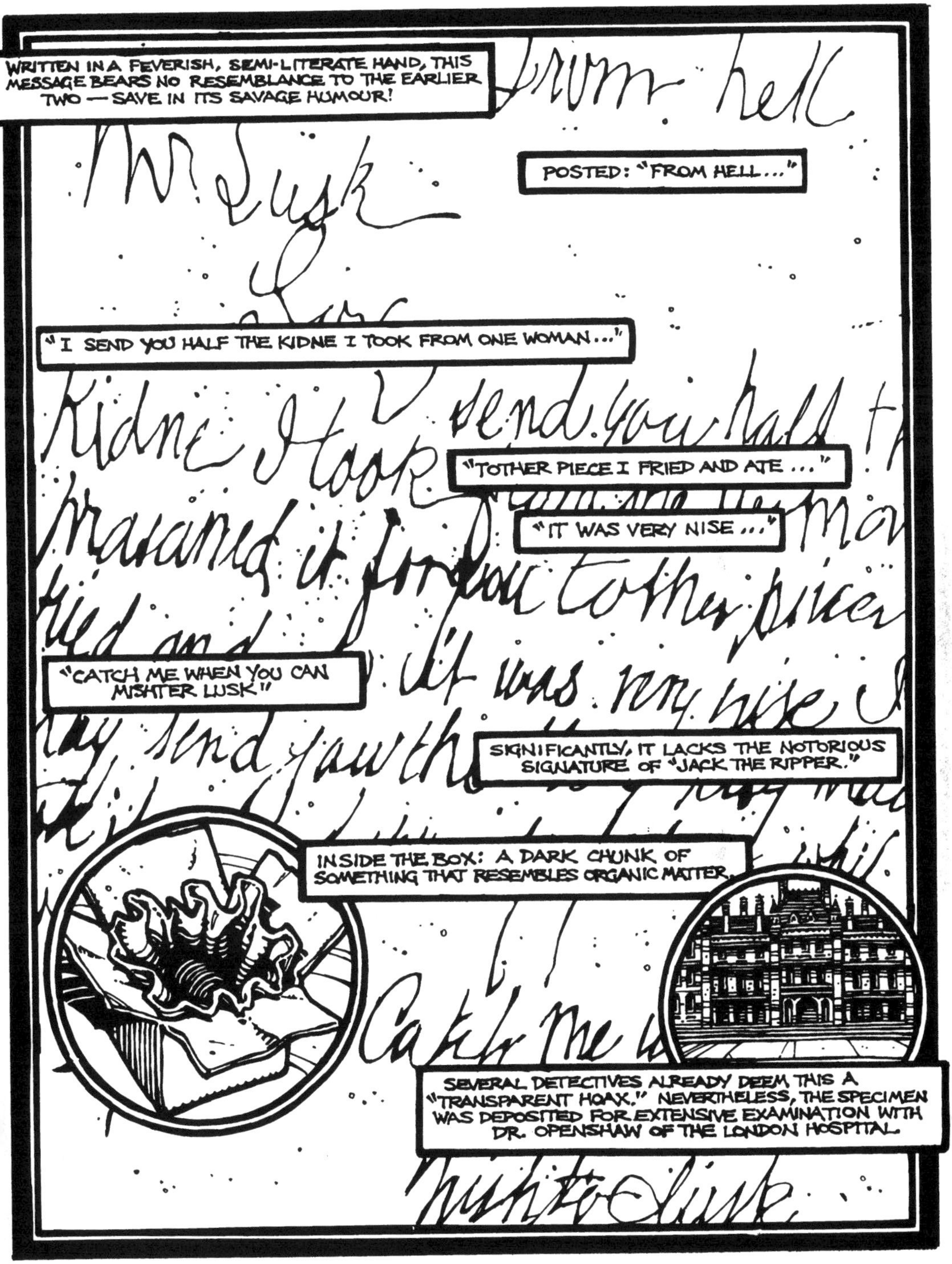
WRITTEN IN A FEVERISH, SEMI-LITERATE HAND, THIS MESSAGE BEARS NO RESEMBLANCE TO THE EARLIER TWO — SAVE IN ITS SAVAGE HUMOUR!
POSTED: "FROM HELL..."
"I SEND YOU HALF THE KIDNE I TOOK FROM ONE WOMAN..."
"TOTHER PIECE I FRIED AND ATE..."
"IT WAS VERY NISE..."
"CATCH ME WHEN YOU CAN MISHTER LUSK"
SIGNIFICANTLY, IT LACKS THE NOTORIOUS SIGNATURE OF "JACK THE RIPPER."
INSIDE THE BOX: A DARK CHUNK OF SOMETHING THAT RESEMBLES ORGANIC MATTER.
SEVERAL DETECTIVES ALREADY DEEM THIS A "TRANSPARENT HOAX." NEVERTHELESS, THE SPECIMEN WAS DEPOSITED FOR EXTENSIVE EXAMINATION WITH DR. OPENSHAW OF THE LONDON HOSPITAL.

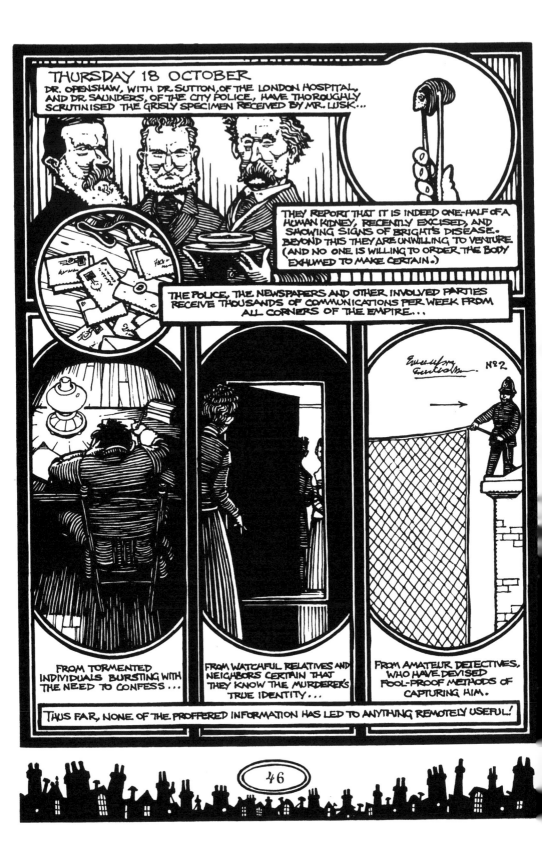

THURSDAY 18 OCTOBER

DR. OPENSHAW, WITH DR. SUTTON, OF THE LONDON HOSPITAL, AND DR. SAUNDERS, OF THE CITY POLICE, HAVE THOROUGHLY SCRUTINISED THE GRISLY SPECIMEN RECEIVED BY MR. LUSK...

THEY REPORT THAT IT IS INDEED ONE-HALF OF A HUMAN KIDNEY, RECENTLY EXCISED, AND SHOWING SIGNS OF BRIGHT'S DISEASE. BEYOND THIS THEY ARE UNWILLING TO VENTURE. (AND NO ONE IS WILLING TO ORDER THE BODY EXHUMED TO MAKE CERTAIN.)

THE POLICE, THE NEWSPAPERS AND OTHER INVOLVED PARTIES RECEIVE THOUSANDS OF COMMUNICATIONS PER WEEK FROM ALL CORNERS OF THE EMPIRE...

FROM TORMENTED INDIVIDUALS BURSTING WITH THE NEED TO CONFESS...

FROM WATCHFUL RELATIVES AND NEIGHBORS CERTAIN THAT THEY KNOW THE MURDERER'S TRUE IDENTITY...

FROM AMATEUR DETECTIVES, WHO HAVE DEVISED FOOL-PROOF METHODS OF CAPTURING HIM.

THUS FAR, NONE OF THE PROFFERED INFORMATION HAS LED TO ANYTHING REMOTELY USEFUL!

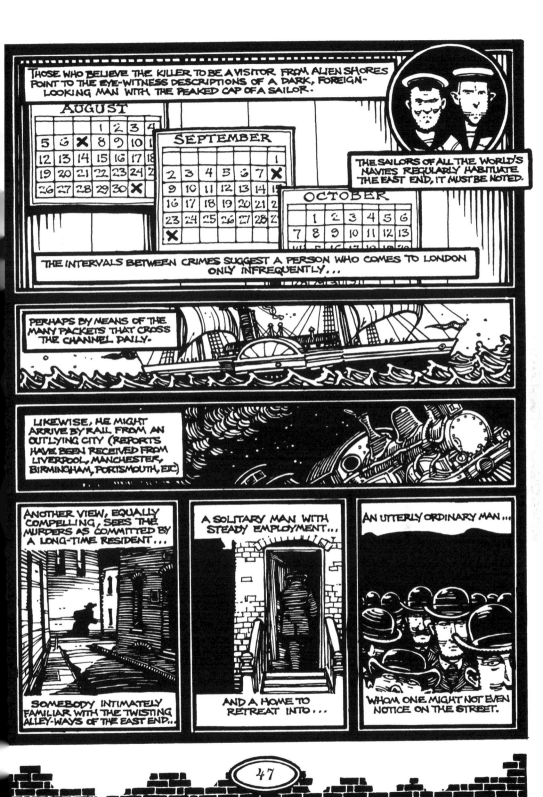

THOSE WHO BELIEVE THE KILLER TO BE A VISITOR FROM ALIEN SHORES POINT TO THE EYE-WITNESS DESCRIPTIONS OF A DARK, FOREIGN-LOOKING MAN WITH THE PEAKED CAP OF A SAILOR.

AUGUST

THE SAILORS OF ALL THE WORLD'S NAVIES REGULARLY HABITUATE THE EAST END, IT MUST BE NOTED.

SEPTEMBER

OCTOBER

THE INTERVALS BETWEEN CRIMES SUGGEST A PERSON WHO COMES TO LONDON ONLY INFREQUENTLY...

PERHAPS BY MEANS OF THE MANY PACKETS THAT CROSS THE CHANNEL DAILY.

LIKEWISE, HE MIGHT ARRIVE BY RAIL FROM AN OUTLYING CITY (REPORTS HAVE BEEN RECEIVED FROM LIVERPOOL, MANCHESTER, BIRMINGHAM, PORTSMOUTH, ETC)

ANOTHER VIEW, EQUALLY COMPELLING, SEES THE MURDERS AS COMMITTED BY A LONG-TIME RESIDENT...

A SOLITARY MAN WITH STEADY EMPLOYMENT...

AN UTTERLY ORDINARY MAN...

SOMEBODY INTIMATELY FAMILIAR WITH THE TWISTING ALLEY-WAYS OF THE EAST END...

AND A HOME TO RETREAT INTO...

WHOM ONE MIGHT NOT EVEN NOTICE ON THE STREET.

MANY OBSERVERS STILL HOLD TO THE IDEA THAT THE KILLER IS A SURGEON OR PHYSICIAN...

OTHERS SAY HE COULD BE A VENGEFUL MAN AFFLICTED WITH DISEASE FROM AN ENCOUNTER WITH A PROSTITUTE....

OR A FATHER OUT TO AVENGE A SON LIKEWISE INFECTED... OR A DAUGHTER TAKEN INTO THE "LIFE..."

A CRAZED "REFORMER" OUT TO DRAW ATTENTION TO EAST-END SQUALOR...

A POLICE-MAN — OR ONE DISGUISED AS SUCH ...

EVEN A WOMAN IS NOT OUT OF THE QUESTION: "JILL THE RIPPER!"

PERHAPS A CAB-DRIVER ...

A "THUGEE" FROM INDIA ...

A TRIBE OF GERMAN HILL PEOPLE WHO "SKIN" THEIR ENEMIES ...

"OPIUM-EATERS" FROM CHINA, WHO HARVEST HUMAN ORGANS...

"SPRING-HEELED JACK," A NOTORIOUS PHANTOM PERSONAGE ...

PRACTITIONERS OF SATANIC "BLACK-MAGIC" RITES ...

REVOLUTIONARY SOCIALISTS OUT TO OVER-THROW THE EMPIRE...

THE "VOO-DOO" CEREMONIES OF WEST-INDIAN SEA-MEN ...

A GREAT APE ESCAPED FROM A TRAVELLING SHOW ...

THURSDAY 31 OCTOBER

OCTOBER HAS PASSED WITH NO FURTHER "RIPPER" CRIMES. THIS CAN ONLY BE ASCRIBED TO THE INCREASED POLICE PRESENCE ON THE STREETS...

AS WELL AS TO THE HUNDREDS OF DETECTIVES AND PRIVATE INDIVIDUALS WHO ARE INVESTIGATING "UNDER-COVER."

THE QUEEN HERSELF HAS VOICED CONCERN FOR IMPROVED CONDITIONS IN THE EAST END.

CITIZENS HAVE LEARNT TO REMAIN INDOORS OF AN EVENING.

THOSE WHO VENTURE ABROAD DO SO IN PAIRS OR GROUPS...

AND OFTEN WELL-ARMED!

THE PROSTITUTES OF THE WHITECHAPEL DISTRICT REMAIN PHILOSOPHICAL ABOUT THEIR LIVES AND FATES:

"WE'RE ALL UP TO NO GOOD, AND NOBODY CARES WHAT BECOMES OF US."

"SUPPOSE I DO GET KILLED," ONE LADY WAS OVER-HEARD TO DECLARE...

"IT WILL BE A GOOD THING FOR ME!"

SEVERAL DETECTIVES NOW FEAR THAT THEY MAY HAVE DONE THEIR JOBS TOO WELL...

AND THAT THE KILLER HAS UP-ROOTED HIMSELF AND MOVED HIS ACTIVITIES TO ANOTHER CITY OR COUNTRY!

FRIDAY 9 NOVEMBER
THE KILLER RETURNED WITH A FURIOUS VENGEANCE THIS MORNING!
THE NEW VICTIM—NAMED MARY JANE KELLY—WAS FOUND IN A ROOM
ON MILLER'S COURT, WHICH IS A FILTHY ALLEY-WAY OFF DORSET STREET.

THE ROOM IS DESIGNATED AS
13 MILLER'S COURT, BUT IS
PART OF THE ROOMING-HOUSE
AT 26 DORSET STREET.

AT ABOUT 10:30 AM, THE
LAND-LORD, MR. McCARTHY,
SENT HIS ASSISTANT ROUND
TO INQUIRE AFTER 35
SHILLINGS IN PAST-DUE RENT.

RECEIVING NO ANSWER FROM
WITHIN, AND FINDING THE
DOOR LOCKED, THE MAN
PEERED THROUGH A BROKEN
WINDOW-PANE.

WHAT HE GLIMPSED IN THE DARK LITTLE ROOM SENT
HIM DASHING IN HORROR FOR THE POLICE.

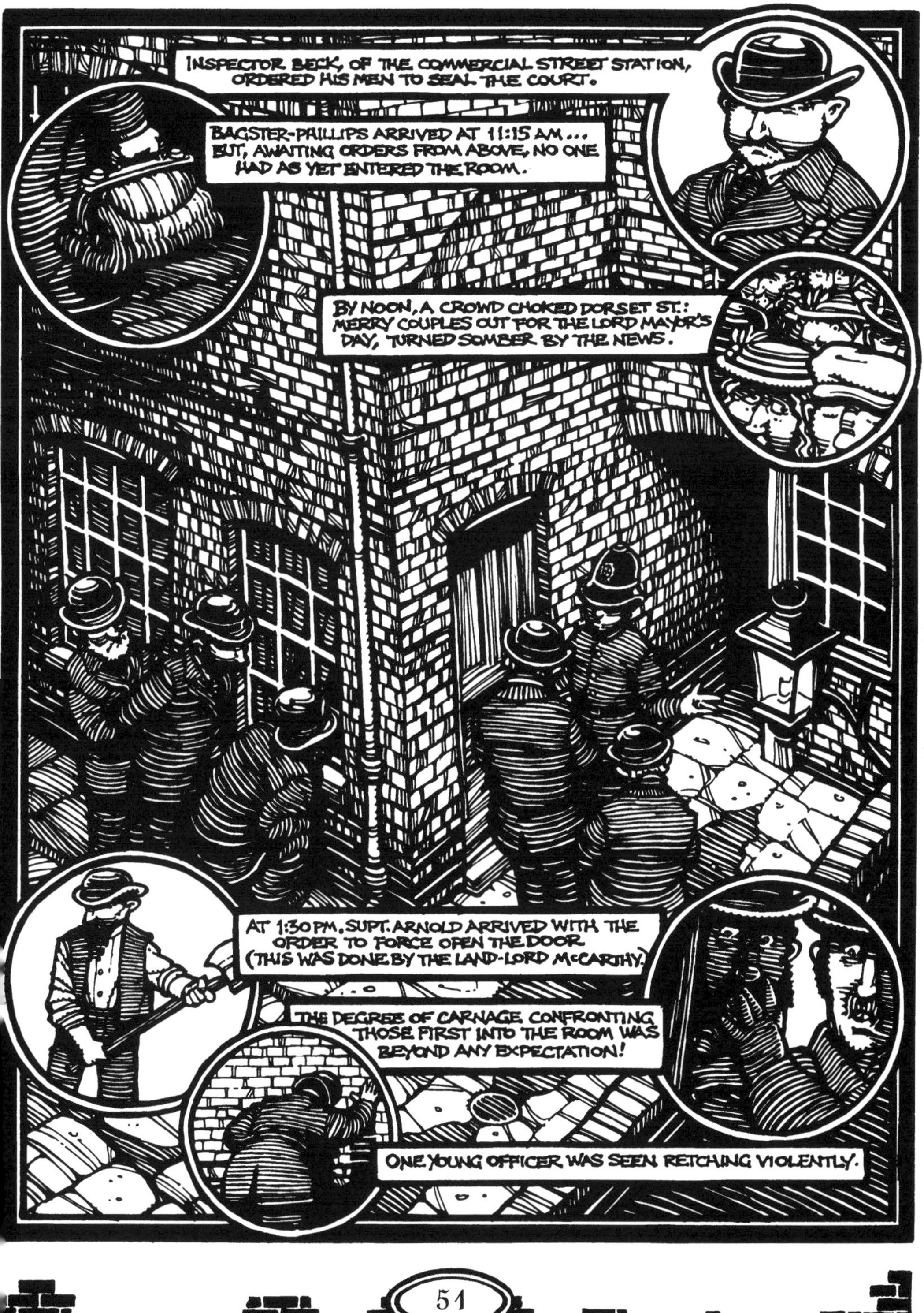
INSPECTOR BECK, OF THE COMMERCIAL STREET STATION, ORDERED HIS MEN TO SEAL THE COURT.
BAGSTER-PHILLIPS ARRIVED AT 11:15 AM... BUT, AWAITING ORDERS FROM ABOVE, NO ONE HAD AS YET ENTERED THE ROOM.
BY NOON, A CROWD CHOKED DORSET ST.: MERRY COUPLES OUT FOR THE LORD MAYOR'S DAY, TURNED SOMBER BY THE NEWS.
AT 1:30 PM, SUPT. ARNOLD ARRIVED WITH THE ORDER TO FORCE OPEN THE DOOR (THIS WAS DONE BY THE LAND-LORD McCARTHY).
THE DEGREE OF CARNAGE CONFRONTING THOSE FIRST INTO THE ROOM WAS BEYOND ANY EXPECTATION!
ONE YOUNG OFFICER WAS SEEN RETCHING VIOLENTLY.

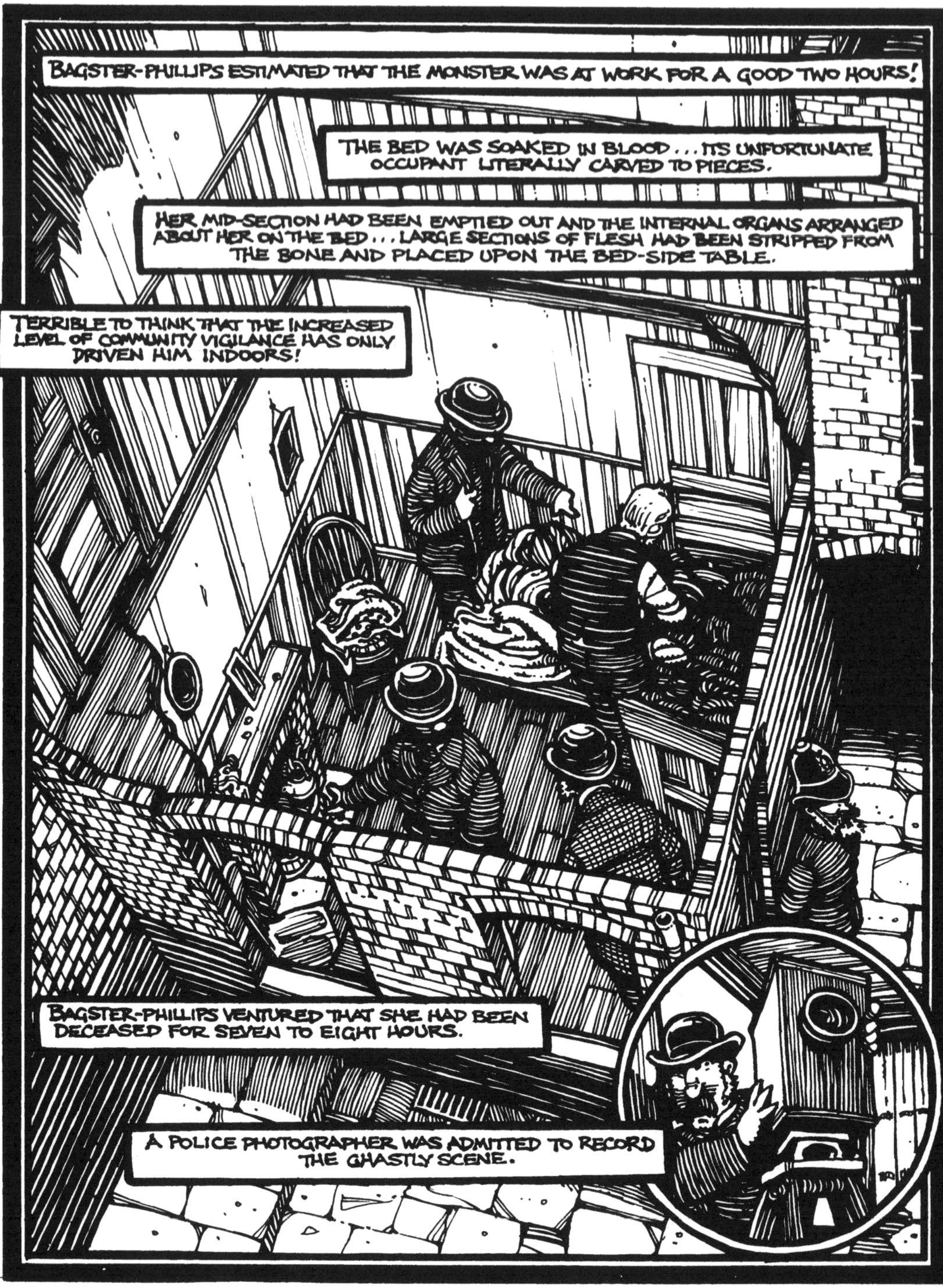
BAGSTER-PHILLIPS ESTIMATED THAT THE MONSTER WAS AT WORK FOR A GOOD TWO HOURS!
THE BED WAS SOAKED IN BLOOD... ITS UNFORTUNATE OCCUPANT LITERALLY CARVED TO PIECES.
HER MID-SECTION HAD BEEN EMPTIED OUT AND THE INTERNAL ORGANS ARRANGED ABOUT HER ON THE BED... LARGE SECTIONS OF FLESH HAD BEEN STRIPPED FROM THE BONE AND PLACED UPON THE BED-SIDE TABLE.
TERRIBLE TO THINK THAT THE INCREASED LEVEL OF COMMUNITY VIGILANCE HAS ONLY DRIVEN HIM INDOORS!
BAGSTER-PHILLIPS VENTURED THAT SHE HAD BEEN DECEASED FOR SEVEN TO EIGHT HOURS.
A POLICE PHOTOGRAPHER WAS ADMITTED TO RECORD THE GHASTLY SCENE.

NO STRUGGLE APPEARED TO HAVE TAKEN PLACE IN THE TINY, SPARSELY-FURNISHED CHAMBER...

IN FACT, THE VICTIM'S CLOTHING LAY NEATLY FOLDED UPON A NEAR-BY CHAIR.

THE BED-SIDE CANDLE HAD APPARENTLY NOT BEEN USED...

BUT IN THE SMALL FIRE-PLACE; THE REMAINS OF AN INTENSE BLAZE...,

SO INTENSE THAT THE SOLDERED JOINTS OF A TEA-KETTLE HANGING THERE HAD MELTED!

AMONG THE ASHES, STILL SMOULDERING, COULD BE FOUND FRAGMENTS OF A WOMAN'S CLOTHING.

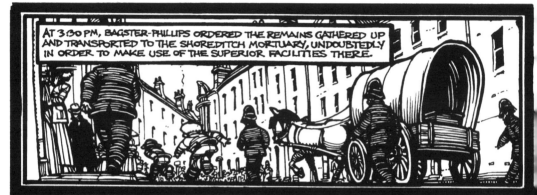

AT 3:30 PM, BAGSTER-PHILLIPS ORDERED THE REMAINS GATHERED UP AND TRANSPORTED TO THE SHOREDITCH MORTUARY, UNDOUBTEDLY IN ORDER TO MAKE USE OF THE SUPERIOR FACILITIES THERE.

HE WAS JOINED BY THE POLICE SURGEON THOS. BOND, AND WITH SEVERAL ASSISTANTS, THEY LABOURED MIGHTILY TO RE-ASSEMBLE THE CORPSE LIKE A JIG-SAW PUZZLE.

CUTS TO HER HANDS INDICATED THAT SHE HAD INDEED OFFERED SOME RESISTANCE TO HER KILLER.

ALL INTERNAL ORGANS WERE ACCOUNTED FOR, SAVE THE WOMAN'S VERY HEART!

THE PHOTOGRAPHER RETURNED... THIS TIME TO PEER INTO HER EYES...

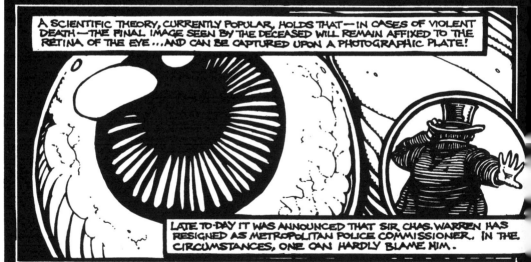

A SCIENTIFIC THEORY, CURRENTLY POPULAR, HOLDS THAT—IN CASES OF VIOLENT DEATH—THE FINAL IMAGE SEEN BY THE DECEASED WILL REMAIN AFFIXED TO THE RETINA OF THE EYE...AND CAN BE CAPTURED UPON A PHOTOGRAPHIC PLATE!

LATE TO-DAY IT WAS ANNOUNCED THAT SIR CHAS. WARREN HAS RESIGNED AS METROPOLITAN POLICE COMMISSIONER. IN THE CIRCUMSTANCES, ONE CAN HARDLY BLAME HIM.

SUNDAY 11 NOVEMBER
A "WHITE-EYED" MAN WITH A BLACKENED FACE, CLAIMING TO BE "JACK THE RIPPER," CAUSED QUITE A STIR THIS EVENING ALONG COMMERCIAL STREET.

HE WAS AT ONCE SET-UPON BY A FURIOUS MOB..., BUT POLICE SAVED HIS LIFE AND BROUGHT HIM TO THE LEMAN ST. STATION.

LYNCH HIM!

YOUNG HOOLIGANS, OFTEN WITH BLACKENED FACES, ARE WELL-KNOWN TO LEAP FROM ALLEY-WAYS, FRIGHTENING PASSERS-BY FOR SPORT...

BUT THIS IS A MAN OF ABOUT 35 YEARS... WHO REFUSES, THUS FAR, TO GIVE HIS NAME.

MONDAY 12 NOVEMBER
THE PUZZLINGLY BRIEF INQUEST UPON MARY JANE KELLY TOOK PLACE THIS MORNING AT THE TOWN HALL IN SHOREDITCH.

THE CORONER, DR. MACDONALD, SPENT A GOOD PART OF THE SESSION IN DEFENSE OF THE DECISION TO REMOVE THE REMAINS TO A DISTRICT APART FROM WHERE THE MURDER TOOK PLACE!

APART FROM HER YOUTHFUL AGE OF 24 YEARS, MARY JANE (OR MARIE JEANETTE) KELLY WAS SEEMINGLY NO DIFFERENT FROM THE WOMEN WHO PRECEDED HER, UNDER THE KILLER'S KNIFE.

A NATIVE OF COUNTY LIMERICK, SHE WAS MARRIED AS A GIRL TO A COLLIER NAMED DAVIES, WHO DIED IN A MINE EXPLOSION.

SOON AFTER, SHE BEGAN HER CAREER OF PROSTITUTION IN A FASHIONABLE LONDON BROTHEL.

SHE HAD LIVED AT VARIOUS TIMES WITH DIFFERENT MEN, HERE AND ON THE CONTINENT, THE LATEST BEING MR. JOS. BARNETT, A LABOURER.

HE TESTIFIED THAT THE TWO OF THEM HAD MOVED INTO THE ROOM AT 13 MILLER'S COURT IN APRIL OF THIS YEAR...

BUT HE HAD MOVED OUT ON 30 OCTOBER, AFTER A VIOLENT QUARREL—DURING WHICH A PANE OF GLASS WAS SHATTERED.

APPARENTLY THE ROOM'S LATCH-KEY HAD BEEN MISSING FOR SEVERAL WEEKS, FORCING THE OCCUPANTS TO SHOOT THE BOLT BY REACHING THROUGH THE BROKEN WINDOW...

YET THE DOOR WAS LEFT SECURELY LOCKED BY THE MURDERER!

SEVERAL TENANTS ON MILLER'S COURT TESTIFIED AS TO THE VICTIM'S COMINGS AND GOINGS ON THE MORNING OF THE MURDER:

MRS. COX, WHO RESIDES AT NUMBER 5, OBSERVED HER EARLIER IN THE EVENING—ABOUT 11:45 PM...

WHEN SHE BROUGHT A CLIENT TO HER ROOM: A SHORT, STOUT MAN WITH A "CARROTY" MOUSTACHE...

AND CLEARLY HEARD HER VOICE THROUGH THE BROKEN WINDOW-PANE, SINGING: "ONLY A VIOLET I PLUCK'D FROM MY MOTHER'S GRAVE."

MISS SARAH LEWIS, WHO ENTERED THE COURT TO VISIT A FRIEND AT ABOUT 2:30 AM...

SAID THAT SHE PASSED A MAN, LOITERING OUTSIDE THE DORSET STREET ENTRANCE...

AND LATER IN THE MORNING—ABOUT 4:00 AM—SHE HEARD A WOMAN'S VOICE CRY: "OH, MURDER!" FROM SOMEWHERE IN THE COURT.

HER TESTIMONY WAS CORROBORATED BY MRS. PRATER, WHO LIVES IN NUMBER 20, DIRECTLY ABOVE THE DECEASED.

SHE HEARD WHAT MUST HAVE BEEN THE SAME CRY OF "MURDER!" AT 3:30 OR 4:00 AM (ABOUT THE HOUR THAT THE DOCTORS PLACE THE TIME OF DEATH).

NEITHER WOMAN ATTACHED ANY IMPORTANCE TO THE CRY, SINCE SUCH EXCLAMATIONS ARE ALL-TOO-COMMON IN THE NEIGHBORHOOD!

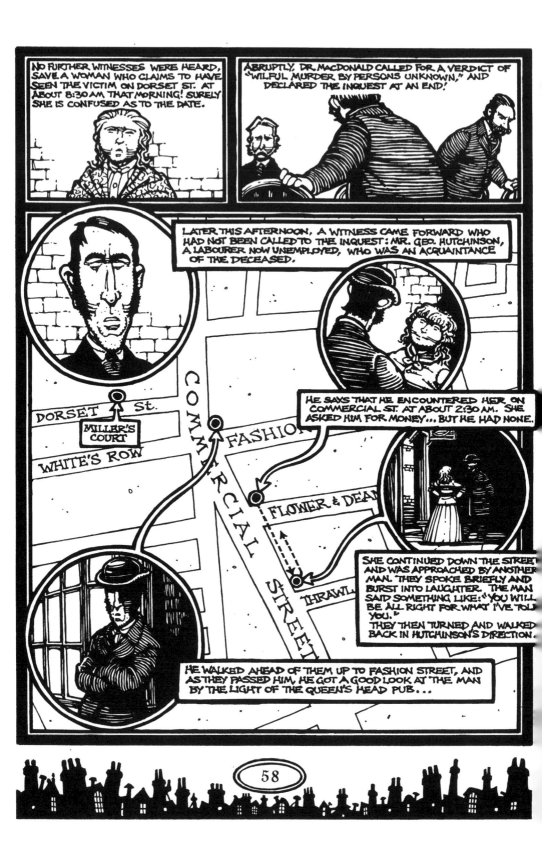

NO FURTHER WITNESSES WERE HEARD, SAVE A WOMAN WHO CLAIMS TO HAVE SEEN THE VICTIM ON DORSET ST. AT ABOUT 8:30 AM THAT MORNING! SURELY SHE IS CONFUSED AS TO THE DATE.

ABRUPTLY, DR. MACDONALD CALLED FOR A VERDICT OF "WILFUL MURDER BY PERSONS UNKNOWN," AND DECLARED THE INQUEST AT AN END!

LATER THIS AFTERNOON, A WITNESS CAME FORWARD WHO HAD NOT BEEN CALLED TO THE INQUEST: MR. GEO. HUTCHINSON, A LABOURER NOW UNEMPLOYED, WHO WAS AN ACQUAINTANCE OF THE DECEASED.

DORSET St.
MILLER'S COURT
WHITE'S ROW
COMMERCIAL STREET
FASHION
FLOWER & DEAN
THRAWL

HE SAYS THAT HE ENCOUNTERED HER ON COMMERCIAL ST. AT ABOUT 2:30 AM. SHE ASKED HIM FOR MONEY... BUT HE HAD NONE.

SHE CONTINUED DOWN THE STREET AND WAS APPROACHED BY ANOTHER MAN. THEY SPOKE BRIEFLY AND BURST INTO LAUGHTER. THE MAN SAID SOMETHING LIKE: "YOU WILL BE ALL RIGHT FOR WHAT I'VE TOLD YOU."
THEY THEN TURNED AND WALKED BACK IN HUTCHINSON'S DIRECTION.

HE WALKED AHEAD OF THEM UP TO FASHION STREET, AND AS THEY PASSED HIM, HE GOT A GOOD LOOK AT THE MAN BY THE LIGHT OF THE QUEEN'S HEAD PUB...

THE MAN, ACCORDING TO HUTCHINSON, WAS MUCH TOO RESPECTABLE-LOOKING FOR THE NEIGHBOURHOOD

"FOREIGN-LOOKING," AND AGED ABOUT 35 YEARS...

A PALE COMPLEXION, DARK HAIR, A SMALL MOUSTACHE.

WEARING A DARK COAT AND TROUSERS, AND A DARK FELT HAT.

HE WORE A HEAVY GOLD WATCH-CHAIN ... AND ON HIS TIE: A JEWELED HORSE-SHOE PIN.

HE CARRIED A SMALL PARCEL, WITH SOME SORT OF STRAP AROUND IT.

HUTCHINSON STOOPED DOWN TO SEE THE MAN'S FACE, AND, "HE LOOKED AT ME STERN."

HE FOLLOWED THE COUPLE ON TO DORSET STREET...

WHERE, AT THE ENTRANCE TO MILLER'S COURT, THEY STOPPED TO TALK AGAIN.

THE DECEASED TOLD HER ESCORT THAT SHE HAD LOST HER HANDKERCHIEF...

WHEREUPON HE PRODUCED A RED ONE FROM HIS POCKET.

SHE THEN SAID: "COME ALONG, MY DEAR, YOU WILL BE COMFORTABLE."

SHE GAVE THE MAN A KISS AND LED HIM INTO THE COURT.

HUTCHINSON THEN WAITED ACROSS THE STREET FOR THEM TO EMERGE...

BUT AFTER ABOUT 45 MINUTES, HE GAVE UP AND WENT HOME.

WEDNESDAY 14 NOVEMBER
THE LATEST MURDER SEEMS TO HAVE BROUGHT THE ENTIRE CITY TO A BOILING-POINT OF HYSTERIA!

TWO DIFFERENT MEN WERE PURSUED BY MOBS TODAY AND ALMOST KILLED BEFORE THEIR RESCUE BY POLICE.

SEVERAL ARRESTS HAVE BEEN MADE— OFTEN UPON VERY FLIMSY INFORMATION, WITH ALL OF THE SUSPECTS EVENTUALLY RELEASED...

INCLUDING THE CURIOUS MAN WITH THE BLACKENED FACE WHOSE NAME IS HOLT AND WHO CLAIMS TO HAVE BEEN SLEUTHING OUT THE "RIPPER" UNDER-COVER!

INSPECTOR ABBERLINE WILL PRIVATELY ADMIT THAT THERE IS LITTLE HIS MEN CAN DO NOW SAVE WAIT FOR THE CRUCIAL PIECE OF INFORMATION TO FALL INTO THEIR HANDS.

WEDNESDAY 21 NOVEMBER

THE STREETS WERE ALIVE THIS MORNING WITH THE NEWS OF ANOTHER MURDER... BUT IT TURNED OUT NOT TO BE THE CASE!

A WOMAN NAMED ANNIE FARMER (WHO IS STILL VERY MUCH ALIVE!) WAS STABBED IN THE THROAT AT A LODGING-HOUSE ON GEORGE STREET. SHE IS CONVINCED THAT SHE WAS ATTACKED BY "JACK THE RIPPER..."

BUT IT SEEMS MORE LIKELY TO HAVE BEEN THE RESULT OF A QUARREL WITH A CLIENT OVER MONEY.

**1889**

TUESDAY 1 JANUARY

IT IS THE BEGINNING OF A NEW YEAR... AND NOW ALMOST TWO MONTHS WITH NO NEW "RIPPER" OUTRAGE.

DETECTIVES FEEL THAT IF THE KILLER HAD MOVED HIS ACTIVITIES TO ANOTHER CITY, WE WOULD HAVE HEARD OF IT BY NOW.

PERHAPS HE IS IN PRISON FOR AN ENTIRELY UNRELATED OFFENSE...OR CONFINED BY HIS FAMILY TO AN ASYLUM FOR THE INSANE...

BUT MOST COMPELLING IS THE CONCLUSION THAT HIS EXTREME DEMENTIA SIMPLY DROVE HIM TO SUICIDE.

INDEED, POLICE ARE NOW LOOKING INTO THE HISTORY OF A YOUNG MAN WHOSE DE-COMPOSED REMAINS WERE DRAGGED FROM THE THAMES JUST YESTERDAY.

HIS NAME WAS DRUITT, A FORMER BARRISTER AND SCHOOL-MASTER, WHO HAD BEEN MISSING SINCE EARLY IN DECEMBER.

A SEARCH OF HIS QUARTERS HAS LED SOME OF THE DETECTIVES TO BELIEVE THAT HE WAS THE KILLER ... BUT, BEYOND THAT THEY REMAIN SILENT.

WEDNESDAY 17 JULY

THE CITY IS ASTIR WITH THE NEWS THAT, AFTER NINE MONTHS, "JACK THE RIPPER" MIGHT BE BACK ABOUT HIS BUSINESS!

THE BODY OF A WOMAN WAS FOUND THIS MORNING AT 1:00 AM, IN CASTLE ALLEY, WHITECHAPEL.

HER THROAT AND ABDOMINAL AREA HAD BEEN TORN BY SEVERAL KNIFE-THRUSTS.

THURSDAY 18 JULY

DR. BAGSTER-PHILLIPS AND DR. BOND HAVE EXAMINED THE BODY, WHICH IS THAT OF ALICE McKENZIE, A PROSTITUTE AGED ABOUT 40 YEARS.

THEY CONCLUDE THAT SHE PERISHED OF STAB WOUNDS, ANGLED DOWNWARD... WITH NO SLICING AND NO ATTEMPT TO OPEN THE BODY. EVIDENTLY NOT THE WORK OF THE SAME MAN.

THE EAST END TO-NIGHT IS RELIEVED BY THE NEWS: NOBODY WANTS TO LIVE THROUGH ANOTHER REIGN OF TERROR.

BUT ARGUMENT AND SPECULATION IN THE CLUBS AND PUBS, IS AS FERVENT AS EVER!

OTHERS MAY CONJURE UP THE FAMILIAR BOGIES... BUT MY PERSONAL VIEW HOLDS THAT THE KILLER WAS NATIVE TO THE DISTRICT (OR A LONG-TIME RESIDENT) WHO LIVED ALONE, KEPT REGULAR HABITS, ATTRACTED LITTLE ATTENTION.

PERHAPS HE WATCHED THESE UNFORTUNATE WOMEN FOR YEARS, WITH EQUAL PARTS OF LUST AND LOATHING... AND FINALLY WITH NO OTHER THOUGHT THAN TO CUT THEM OPEN!

AS TO HIS REASONS... WHO WILL EVER KNOW?

HE WOULD APPROACH EACH VICTIM AT A TIME WHEN SHE WAS MOST HELPLESS FROM DRINK AND DESPERATE FOR MONEY...

AND, AT THE FIRST POSSIBLE MOMENT, HE STRANGLED HER TO DEATH. (THE POST-MORTEM REPORTS FOR MOST OF THE WOMEN MENTION THAT THEIR FACES WERE SWOLLEN OR DISCOLOURED—FAMILIAR SIGNS OF STRANGULATION!)

HE THEN COULD PERFORM HIS MUTILATIONS WITH A MINIMUM OF BLOOD-FLOW...

AND, AS THE ENTIRE WORLD WITNESSED, HE BECAME MORE PROFICIENT WITH EACH VENTURE!

FINALLY, AT MILLER'S COURT, HE HAD THE CHANCE TO CARRY HIS DESIRES TO THEIR LIMIT...

AND YET HE WAS NOT SATISFIED... PERHAPS HE WOULD NEVER BE!

AND SO, I PREFER TO BELIEVE THAT THEN, AS A TORMENTED INDIVIDUAL, HE ARRANGED A QUIET END FOR HIMSELF... CARRYING HIS SECRETS WITH HIM.

HIS VICTIMS ARE LIKEWISE SILENT IN THEIR ANONYMOUS RESTS.

ALL HUMAN ENDEAVOR, IT SEEMS, MUST CRUMBLE AGAINST THE ALL-PERVASIVE SILENCE OF THE GRAVE...

WHICH IS WHY I BELIEVE THAT THE MYSTERIES SURROUNDING THESE CRIMES WILL NEVER BE PENETRATED...

BUT NEVERTHELESS WILL REVERBERATE FORWARD THROUGH THE CENTURIES!

End